Financial Reporting 1983–84:

A Survey of UK Published Accounts

Financial Reporting 1983–84:
A Survey of UK Published Accounts

Edited by

D. J. Tonkin

Special Adviser to
The Institute of Chartered Accountants of Scotland

and

L. C. L. Skerratt

Spicer and Pegler Professor of Accounting,
University of Durham

Foreword by Sir John Grenside

The Institute of Chartered Accountants

in England and Wales

Chartered Accountants' Hall,

Moorgate Place, London EC2P 2BJ

1983

ACKNOWLEDGEMENTS

This publication is sponsored by The Institute of Chartered Accountants in England and Wales, and does not necessarily represent the view of the Institute.

The Institute and the Editors gratefully acknowledge the assistance of all concerned in the preparation of the work.

Each section is researched and written by individual contributors. The function of the Editorial Board is to assist the Editors in reviewing the first drafts submitted by the contributors and to deal with broad policy matters. Co-ordination and planning are undertaken by the Editors.

Contributors

The text was prepared and written by:

E. C. M. Barnes, FCA	Manager of the National Technical Department, Spicer and Pegler, London.
P. D. Bougen, BA MPhil	Lecturer in Accounting, University of Leeds.
J. P. Carty, BSc(Econ) MA FCA	James Carty & Co.
C. J. Cowton, BA ACIS	University of Wales Institute of Science and Technology.
C. R. Emmanuel, BSc(Econ) MA PhD ACIS	University College of Wales, Aberystwyth.
R. H. Gray, MA(Econ) FCA	University College of North Wales, Bangor.
S. J. Gray, BEc PhD FCCA	Professor of Accountancy, University of Glasgow.
C. J. Napier, MA MSc ACA	London School of Economics, University of London.
J. H. Plowdon, BSc ACA	Thomson McLintock & Co./ K.M.G., Edinburgh.
C. B. Roberts, MSc	Research Assistant, University of Glasgow.
D. M. C. E. Steen, MA FCA	Partner, Peat, Marwick, Mitchell & Co., London
D. P. Tweedie, BCom PhD CA	Partner, Thomson McLintock & Co./K.M.G., Edinburgh; and Visiting Professor, International Centre for Research in Accounting, University of Lancaster.
R. M. Wilkins, FCA	Senior Manager, Peat, Marwick, Mitchell & Co., London.
R. A. Wyld, CA (Canada)	National Director of Audit Research, Touche Ross & Co., London.

Collection of accounts

Paula Gray, of Spicer and Pegler, London, undertook the crucial task of collecting and distributing sets of accounts of listed companies in time for the research to begin in early July. Clare Roberts, of Glasgow University, performed the same task for the unlisted companies.

Copying and reproduction

FOREWORD
by
SIR JOHN GRENSIDE

Financial reporting is at present in a state of flux. There are continuing pressures for increased disclosures in company annual reports and a notable example of this is the 1981 Companies Act, which is now having a major impact on reporting by all UK companies. Apart from the increased disclosures required, company accounts on the new basis have what is to many a new unfamiliar look, both in layout and terminology, as they must accord with the prescribed formats that stem from the EEC 4th Directive.

At the same time as these major changes in the law are taking effect there is renewed debate about the most appropriate way to reflect the impact of changing prices, as the planned review of SSAP 16 takes its course. In addition, after a lengthy development period, an important standard on "Foreign Currency Translation" (SSAP 20) was issued last April, and there are standards pending on major topics such as leasing, pension costs and business combinations.

In the light of these developments, it is important that there should be an up-to-date reference work available of what companies are actually doing in practice. The Institute's annual survey of 300 sets of published accounts fulfils this purpose admirably. As Sir Ronald Leach said in his foreword to the 1st Edition of this survey 15 years ago: "This demand for more information has presented many difficulties and the survey tries to show how various companies have attempted to solve some of the problems which have arisen."

This year the survey is adopting a new approach, concentrating more on the most topical areas, such as those referred to above. For instance some 20 companies in the survey have chosen to follow the detailed 1981 Act requirements a year in advance of it becoming mandatory.

Apart from this greater in-depth selectivity, this year's survey also analyses company reporting practices between large listed, medium listed and large unlisted companies and this should make it a more useful practical tool.

With the vastly greater quantity of information given in today's company reports, it is all too easy to slip below the highest standards of quality and I believe this year's survey will continue to assist in the perennial search for clear, concise and informative financial reporting.

Sir John Grenside

EDITORIAL INTRODUCTION

This is the fifteenth annual survey in this series. The work is based on the financial statements of 300 industrial and commercial companies issued during the year to 30 June 1983. Details of the sample selection procedure are contained in Appendix 1 at the end of the survey. The primary purpose of the survey is to give a factual report of financial disclosure practices of the companies in the sample. However, financial disclosure practice does not exist in a vacuum, and the survey evaluates it against the background of disclosure rules and proposals which exist amongst substantial parts of the financial community. This background includes articles published in the accounting and financial literature (both professional and academic).

OBJECTIVES

This edition of the survey marks an important change in editorial objectives. Each of the previous fourteen editions has provided a comprehensive survey of all aspects of the financial reporting practices of those companies included in the sample. Some aspects of financial reporting practice change more slowly than others. The editors have decided to reflect this differing pattern of change by reducing the frequency with which the relatively static aspects are surveyed.

Two implications follow from this new editorial objective. Firstly, individual editions will no longer provide a comprehensive survey of financial reporting practice. Each will contain a cumulative contents list indicating where the latest analysis of any specific aspect of financial reporting practice can be found. Secondly, relatively greater resources will be devoted to the analysis of the more rapidly changing aspects and so lead to a more relevant and interesting annual survey. For example, in the current edition, there is a seven-fold increase in the number of analysis tables addressing various aspects of foreign currency reporting.

The implementation of this change in objectives is based on the editors' classification of aspects of financial reporting practice into three classes which will be surveyed on one-year, three-year and five-year cycles. This classification will change over time to reflect changes in the relative importance of accounting issues.

Additionally, the opportunity has been taken to change the basis on which the sample companies are selected and analysed. The new basis adopts a three-way classification into large listed, medium listed and large unlisted companies. This classification is reflected in the analysis tables of each section.

Details of the sample selection basis are set out in Appendix 1 at the end of the survey. Finally, the statistical significance of the differences between the three categories of company is reported in a note to each analysis table.

STRUCTURE

For ease of reference, the structure of each section is standardised as follows:

Introduction

This heading covers a brief statement of the subject matter of the section and sets out to indicate, again briefly, why the subject is sufficiently important to warrant analysis in this survey.

Requirements

This heading covers the various influences on financial disclosure practice examined in the section. The material is divided according to source, eg statutory requirements, standard accounting practice and Stock Exchange requirements. The Requirements section gives only a broad outline of the subject area to provide a background for the Analysis section; it does not aim to be comprehensive.

Analysis

This heading covers the presentation of the analysis tables. Although much of this section is factual, some element of judgement is necessary for useful analysis. The choice of issues on which a section focuses, together with the choice of definitions in a table, is based on the contributor's judgement; a contributor's commentary on the relationship between current disclosure practice and either (a) requirements or (b) past disclosure practice, will also require judgement.

Examples

This heading covers extracts from the accounts of particular companies, illustrating some stated aspect of the disclosure practices of the sample companies.

Further reading

This heading covers a selected list of topical references relevant to the material presented in the Requirements section. Additionally, the Library of the Institute of Chartered Accountants in England and Wales prepares reading lists on several of the subjects covered by the survey. The corresponding reading list is identified under this heading for the benefit of those who wish to study the subject further.

CONTENTS

	Page
Acknowledgements	v
Foreword *Sir John Grenside*	vii
Editorial introduction	ix
Recent developments *E. C. M. Barnes*	1
Company law	1
Companies Act 1981	1
Companies Act 1981 and SSAP 9	3
Companies (Beneficial Interests) Act 1983	3
Companies (Accounts) Regulations 1982	3
Employment Act 1982	4
EC Seventh Company Law Directive	4
UK accounting standards	4
The standard setting process	4
Public sector liaison group	5
UK Statements of Standard Accounting Practice	5
UK Exposure Drafts	5
UK Discussion Papers	7
Current cost accounting	8
Examples	9
Associated companies *R. A. Wyld*	15
Introduction	15
Requirements	15
Analysis	17
Associated company treatment	17
Reasons given for not using associated company treatment	18
Disclosure of attributable results of associated companies	18
Associated companies in the consolidated balance sheet	19
Definition of an associated company	19
Conclusion	20
Examples	21
Further reading	22
Current cost accounting *J. H. Plowdon and D. P. Tweedie*	23
Introduction	23
Requirements	24
Statutory requirements	24
Standard accounting practice	24
Analysis	26
Introduction	26
The impact of current cost adjustments on historical cost profit before taxation	26
Failure to provide current cost statements	29
Problems of companies complying with the standard	33
Bases adopted for assessing current cost valuations and adjustments	36
General	39
Example	40
Further reading	47

	Page
Fixed assets *J. P. Carty*	49
Introduction	49
Requirements	49
Statutory requirements	49
Standard accounting practice	50
International standards	50
Analysis	51
Presentation	51
Classification of fixed assets	51
Valuation of fixed assets in HCA	52
Government grants	54
Directors' statements on the market value of property	54
Investment property	56
Valuation of fixed assets in CCA	57
Depreciation	58
Asset lives for current cost accounts	61
Examples	62
Further reading	63
Foreign currencies *S. J. Gray and C. B. Roberts*	65
Introduction	65
Requirements	66
Statutory requirements	66
Standard accounting practice	67
International accounting standards	68
Analysis	68
Accounting policies	68
Translation methods	69
Treatment of exchange differences	70
Impact of exchange differences	76
Disclosure of additional information	78
Summary and conclusions	81
Examples	81
Further reading	85
Group Accounts *D. M. C. E. Steen and R. M. Wilkins*	87
Introduction	87
Requirements	87
Form of group accounts	87
Accounting dates	88
Minority interests	88
Changes in the composition of a group	89
Treatment of goodwill	90
Holding company accounts	91
Analysis	92
Exclusion from consolidation	92
Accounting dates	93
Minority interests	95
Changes in the composition of a group	96
Treatment of goodwill	99
Investments and other interests in subsidiaries in the accounts of holding companies	101

		Page
Examples		103
Further reading		106

Pension costs   *C. J. Napier* — 107
Introduction		107
Requirements		108
Statutory requirements		108
Standard accounting practice		108
International standards		109
Analysis		110
Number of items disclosed		110
Pension expense		112
Actuarial involvement		112
Miscellaneous disclosures		114
Examples		115
Further reading		116

Political and charitable contributions   *C. J. Cowton* — 117
Introduction		117
Requirements		117
Analysis		117
Ease of locating information		118
Compliance and content		118
Voluntary additional disclosure		120
Examples		122
Further reading		123

Research and development   *R. H. Gray* — 125
Introduction		125
Requirements		126
Statutory requirements		126
Standard accounting practice		127
International accounting standards		128
Analysis		129
Involvement in R & D activity		129
Incidence of R & D by industry sector		130
Accounting policies disclosed		131
Method of disclosure of details of R & D activities		132
Disclosure of R & D written off		133
Size of R & D expenditure		133
Apparent failures to comply with requirements		134
Examples		135
Further reading		137

Segmental disclosure   *C. R. Emmanuel* — 139
Introduction		139
Requirements		139
Statutory requirements		139
Evaluation of changes		140
Analysis		140
Disclosure practice		140

	Page
Presentation adopted	143
Reasons given for not meeting the legal requirements	146
Examples	146
Further reading	149
Value added *P. D. Bougen*	151
Introduction	151
Requirements	152
Analysis	153
Value added statements provided	153
Presentation	154
Audit	155
Basis of calculation of value added	155
Distribution of value added	157
Examples	160
Further reading	163
Appendix 1	165
Introduction	165
Sample selection criteria	165
Statistical significance of the tables	165
Companies included in this survey	166
Appendix 2	170
Cumulative contents list	170

RECENT DEVELOPMENTS

E. C. M. Barnes

COMPANY LAW

Companies Act 1981

1 Appointed day

As mentioned in the previous edition of this survey, the appointed day for Part I to come into operation was 15 June 1982. The major revisions to accounts presentation and disclosure, in particular the prescribed formats for profit and loss accounts and balance sheets, are thus mandatory for accounting periods commencing on or after that date. Thus although a minority of companies have chosen to apply the new rules to earlier periods, the great majority of the financial statements which are the basis for this edition have been drawn up under the "old" Schedule 8 to the 1948 Companies Act which is now Schedule 8A.

2 Implementation of the new rules

The published financial statements of those companies which have adopted the new disclosure rules give some indication of the implementation of the new rules in practice. The accounts of 36 such companies have been examined; these companies were not selected in any systematic basis and were not confined to the usual survey sample. Four of these companies fell within the scope of these new requirements, whereas the remaining 32 companies adopted them voluntarily.

(a) 28 companies adopted the vertical "Operational" profit and loss account format (Format 1) and 8 companies adopted the vertical "Type of expenditure" format (Format 2). An example of each is provided later in this section.

(b) Only one company adopted the horizontal balance sheet format (Format 2). Of the remaining companies adopting the vertical format (Format 1), 29 drew a total immediately before "Capital and reserves" (Heading K) and 6 companies drew a total after "Total assets less current liabilities" (Heading G). One example of each of these three is provided later in this section.

(c) The Act requires directors to adapt the format headings and sub-headings to which an Arabic number is assigned where the special nature of the business requires such adaptation. Furthermore, balance sheets and profit and loss accounts may also include items not otherwise covered in the format adopted. Having regard to either or both of these rules, companies have indeed used headings and sub-headings not included in the formats.

Terms employed in balance sheets include:
"Assets held for finance leasing"
"Advance payments against merchandise"
"Deposits at short call"
"Acceptance credits"
"Vehicle deposits with manufacturers"
"Disposal of businesses"
"Plantations"

1

"Deferred repairs"
"Cylinders"
"Vehicles, casks and sundry equipment"
Terms employed in profit and loss accounts include:
"Occupancy costs"
"Repairs, renewals and maintenance of properties, fixtures, fittings and equipment"
"Research and development"
"Exploration expenditure"
"Re-organisation and severance costs"
"Royalties receivable"
"Distribution and selling costs"
"Production taxes"
"Release of investment grants".

(d) If, in the opinion of the directors, a company carries on businesses of two or more substantially different classes, there must be disclosed the turnover and the profit or loss before taxation attributable to each class. The disclosure is to be made in the notes to the accounts rather than, under the earlier rules, in the directors' report. 28 companies disclosed turnover on this basis. Of those 28 companies, 21 disclosed the attributable profit or loss before taxation (although in doing so 15 included group finance or other central costs as separate headings in the analysis), 4 companies disclosed an analysis of attributable profit or loss before finance costs and 3 companies made no disclosure of the attributable profit or loss.

(e) The Act requires disclosure, where assets other than stocks and work in progress have been included at a valuation other than on historical cost accounting principles, of the comparable historical cost amounts for both written down value and aggregate depreciation. 28 of the companies examined included revalued tangible fixed assets. 16 of those companies adopted the requirement, 2 other companies did so partially in disclosing the historic cost but not the aggregate depreciation, and 10 did not.

(f) Disclosure is required of any material difference between the purchase price or production cost of year end stocks, calculated by reference to the FIFO, LIFO, weighted average price or similar methods, and their current replacement cost. Stocks were included in the balance sheets of 33 of the 36 sets of company accounts examined. 20 companies made no disclosure, 2 companies stated that there was no material difference and the accounts of 1 company were prepared on the current cost basis. 10 companies disclosed differences, some apparently immaterial, as follows:

Balance sheet value £m	Replacement cost £m
777·0	1311·2
60·6	73·0
302·1	305·6
242·2	245·6
163·3	164·8
41·065	41·335
14·862	14·935
4·803	4·866
4·552	4·582
6·666	6·680

2

(g) In complying with the requirement to disclose the average number of employees within categories to be determined by the directors, with regard to the manner in which the company is organised, 15 companies made a disclosure by reference to the principal activities, 6 disclosed by reference to geographical areas, 3 companies gave information on both the preceding bases, 3 companies disclosed by reference to the "operational" profit and loss account (i.e. production, distribution and administration) and 3 companies distinguished between managerial and hourly paid staff. 1 company stated that all employees fell into a single category and 5 companies made no disclosure.

Companies Act 1981 and SSAP 9

In July 1983 the ASC released to the press the text of its letter to a representative of the contracting industry concerning the conflict between the requirements of SSAP 9 "Stocks and work in progress" and the relevant historical cost accounting rule in the Companies Act 1981. The problem was seen to be that the requirement of SSAP 9 for the inclusion of attributable profit in year end long term work in progress may not be consistent with the requirement of the Companies Act 1981 which states that current assets are to be valued at purchase price or production cost or lower net realisable value.

The letter announced that a proposed ASC statement on the conflict would not be issued because:

(a) the ASC has a policy of not issuing interpretations; and
(b) the text of the proposed statement had become unwieldy as a result of attempts to accommodate the views of interested parties.

The letter confirmed that the ASC had concluded that SSAP 9 should remain in force without amendment. The letter also states "Any company which is concerned about the conflict with the Companies Act 1981 is of course free, and even encouraged, to obtain its own legal advice".

Companies (Beneficial Interests) Act 1983

The effect of the Act is to interpret retrospectively certain references to beneficial interests in the 1948 and 1980 Acts. Prior to the 1983 Act, the effect of section 27 of the 1948 Act could have been to undermine the title to shares in a company where they were held by a subsidiary as the corporate trustee of the company's pension scheme; this is no longer the case. Similarly, the effect of paragraphs 15 and 60 of the old and new 8th Sschedules respectively could have been to require disclosure of the holding in a note to the accounts; this is also no longer the case. The new Act also remedies a matter concerned with employees' share schemes. Section 37 of the 1980 Act provides that where shares in a public company are acquired with the company's financial assistance, they must, if the company has a beneficial interest, be cancelled or disposed of within a year.

In the words of the Government spokesman, the purpose of the Act is ". . . to enable people to continue doing what has been done without question for many years. . .".

The Companies (Accounts) Regulations 1982)

This Statutory Instrument amends the Companies Act 1967 with the following effects in respect of accounts approved by directors on or after 31 December 1982:

3

(a) A banded table of directors' emoluments need not be disclosed if aggregate emoluments do not exceed £60,000 (formerly £40,000) and the company is neither a holding nor a subsidiary company.

(b) The number of employees earning more than £30,000 (formerly £20,000) is to be disclosed in bands of £5,000.

The Employment Act 1982

Section 1 requires that companies with more than 250 employees in the United Kingdom must disclose in directors' reports the action taken during the financial year to introduce, maintain or develop arrangements aimed at:

(a) providing them systematically with information on matters of concern to them;

(b) consulting them or their representatives on a regular basis so that their views can be taken into account in making decisions which are likely to affect their interests;

(c) encouraging their involvement in the company's performance through an employees' share scheme or by some other means; and

(d) making them aware of the financial and economic factors affecting the performance of the company

A Statutory Instrument, The Employment Act 1982 (Commencement) Order 1982, has been published which requires that the new disclosures be made in directors' reports attached to accounts for financial years commencing on or after 1 January 1983.

EC Seventh Company Law Directive

The Seventh Directive, on consolidated accounts, was adopted in June 1983. It is referred to in this survey in the section "Group accounts".

Member states will have until the end of 1987 to pass the necessary laws to implement the Directive and until 1990 to apply the Directive to undertakings concerned. The Department of Trade will publish in due course a consultative document on the implementation of the Directive in the UK.

UK ACCOUNTING STANDARDS

The Standard Setting Process

The Accounting Standards Committee (ASC) issued a report in May 1983 to present the conclusions reached following a review of the standard setting process. The review was undertaken:

(a) to develop certain recommendations contained in the Watts Report ("Setting Accounting Standards", 1981) which was referred to in the 1981–82 edition;

(b) to seek ways by which the standard setting process could be shortened whilst ensuring that the resultant standards command general support; and

(c) to consider whether there was a need for alternative or new types of pronouncement.

The principal conclusions in the report were:

(a) Future accounting standards (SSAPs) should deal only with matters of major and fundamental importance affecting the generality of companies. They will therefore be few in number.

(b) A new category of final pronouncement, the Statement of Recommended Practice (SORP), is to be introduced. SORP's will be issued to cover matters which do not meet the new criteria which are seen as warranting a standard. Although compliance with SORP's will be encouraged, they will not be mandatory. It is expected that a SORP will be published on the subject of "Pension scheme accounts".

"Franked SORPs" will be produced to deal with topics of limited application, for example industry specific matters. Their development will be overseen and reviewed by the ASC but they will be published by the industry concerned.

(c) A new form of consultative document, the Statement of Intent (SOI), is also to be introduced to enable the ASC to indicate at an early stage how it proposes to deal with a particular accounting matter.

The ASC also indicated in the report that it has decided to continue the practice of not issuing interpretations of accounting standards.

Public Sector Liaison Group

In September 1983, the ASC announced the formation of a new Public Sector Liaison Group to contribute to the further development of accounting and financial report standards and procedures in the public sector – nationalised industries, local authorities, the National Health Service and central government.

UK Statements of Standard Accounting Practice

At the time of writing, one new accounting standard has been issued since the previous edition. SSAP 20 "Foreign currency translation" was published in April 1983 and is to be regarded as standard in respect of financial statements relating to accounting periods commencing on or after 1 April 1983. Its requirements are referred to in this survey in the section "Foreign currencies".

UK Exposure Drafts

Two exposure drafts have been issued since the previous edition.

1 ED 32 "Disclosure of pension information in company accounts"

ED 32 was published in May 1983 for comment by 30 November 1983. The proposals in this exposure draft are referred to in this survey in the section "Pension costs".

2 ED 33 "Accounting for deferred tax"

ED 33 was published in June 1983 for comment also by 30 November 1983.

The proposals in the exposure draft for the revision of SSAP 15 take account of:

(a) the new tax disclosure requirements in the Companies Act 1981;
(b) the provisions of the Finance Act 1981 whereby stock relief became effectively a permanent, rather than a timing, difference – the exposure draft states that it incorporates the substance of the ASC Guidance Note on this matter issued in November 1981; and
(c) comments received on the working of SSAP 15.

The main proposals, based on comments received, and the reasons for them are set out below.

(a) While there would be no change to the fundamental premise of SSAP 15, that deferred tax should be accounted for on the basis of partial provision using the liability method, there should be a change of emphasis from *"do provide unless. . ."* to *"provide to the extent that it is probable that a liability will crystallise and do not provide to the extent that it is probable that a liability will not crystallise"*. The ASC consider that, under SSAP 15, some boards of directors wishing to provide deferred tax in full have considered that they are not required to undertake an appraisal of the future, based on the information available and their intentions. This, the ASC believes, has led to a considerable flexibility in approach and, in a number of cases, to the creation of unrealistically prudent deferred tax provisions.
(b) Rather than giving a minimum future appraisal period of three years (which the preface to the exposure draft suggests has become, in practice, a maximum) it is proposed simply that companies should assess the likelihood of any liability crystallising in the light of their own particular circumstances. In some cases this will entail looking more than three years ahead.
(c) The requirement to disclose the full potential deferred tax liability in a note produced comments that this is misleading if there is no prospect of the liability crystallising. However, given the practical difficulties of analysing the full potential liability into its "remote" and "not remote" components and the interest expressed by investment analysts among others in "fully taxed" earnings, the ASC intend to retain the requirement. It is suggested, nevertheless, that companies who feel able to do so may analyse the full potential liability into its "remote" and "not remote" components, if they so wish.

The remaining exposure drafts in issue are:

1 ED 28 "Accounting for Petroleum Revenue Tax"

The period for comment on this exposure draft ended on 8 June 1981. As a result of changes in the tax legislation, no further work is being undertaken on this issue.

2 ED 29 "Accounting for leases and hire purchase contracts"

The exposure period for ED 29 ended on 31 March 1982. Its proposals are referred to in this survey in the section "Leasing and hire purchase".

3 ED 30 "Accounting for goodwill"

The proposals in ED 30 were described in Section 1 "Recent Developments" in the previous edition of this survey.

The exposure period ended on 31 March 1983. In July 1983 the ASC announced that the majority view of commentators on ED 30 was that goodwill should be written off immediately on acquisition against reserves. However a significant minority had underlined the need to allow the option of amortisation. Immediate write-off is a much more common method in practice in the UK than amortisation; in the USA and Canada, however, amortisation is mandatory. EC legislation and the forthcoming international standard will allow both methods. On pragmatic grounds the ASC therefore decided to retain the option of amortisation in developing a standard requiring the elimination of goodwill, to be achieved normally by immediate write-off against reserves. The ASC will give guidance regarding the period over which the amortisation should take place. No exemptions for special types of businesses are envisaged.

4 ED 31 "Accounting for acquisitions and mergers"

The period for comment on this exposure draft ended on 31 March 1983. The proposals in ED 31, and also the requirements of a Statutory Instrument laying down disclosure requirements for companies taking advantage of Section 37 of the Companies Act 1981, were described in Section 1 "Recent developments" in the previous edition of this survey.

UK Discussion Papers

The ASC has issued two discussion papers which examine some problems which have arisen in the application of two accounting standards. The forewords to both papers state that their publication does not necessarily mean that the respective standards will be revised; they are not statements of intent.

1 "A review of SSAP 6 – Extraordinary items and prior year adjustments"

The ASC working party which prepared the discussion paper is concerned with the considerable inconsistency in the treatment of some apparently similar items in the accounts of different companies. They point in particular to the evidence in previous editions of this survey of a variety of approach in disclosing, for example, redundancy costs or profits or losses on sales of fixed assets as either exceptional or extraordinary items (see "Financial Reporting 1982–83", page 76, Table 9.1). Although SSAP 6 gives some examples of items which might be regarded as exceptional or extraordinary, it also emphasises that the classification of items as extraordinary will depend on the particular circumstances – "what is extraordinary in one business will not necessarily be extraordinary in another". The working party consider that this statement has been interpreted as permitting some of the inconsistencies.

The discussion document includes the following suggestions:

(a) The definitions in the standard should be supplemented by a list defining by nature whether items are *normally* to be treated as an undisclosed credit or charge, an exceptional item, an extraordinary item or a reserve movement. The working party recognise that such lists, of which it gives examples, cannot be exhaustive and also acknowledges that there will be situations wherein the treatment proposed is not appropriate. In these cases, the reasons for the alternative treatment adopted would be disclosed.

(b) The words "expected not to recur frequently or regularly" should be deleted from the standard's definition of extraordinary items. Alternatively the standard should emphasise that it is the event or transaction leading to the extraordinary item which should not recur, not the category of transaction.

(c) Reorganisation costs not involving the termination of a business primarily represent an effort to keep the business running or to increase efficiency. They should therefore be regarded as coming within the ordinary activities and charged against profit before tax, disclosed as an exceptional item if material. In contrast, the costs of closing a significant and identifiable part of the business should be treated as extraordinary.

(d) Whenever the movements on the reserve to which retained profit is added are shown other than as the bottom line of the profit and loss account, a statement analysing those movements, and not merely prior year adjustments, should immediately follow the profit and loss account. The working party have identified a trend to relegating reserve movements, despite their importance, to the notes to the accounts.

2 "A review of SSAP 12 – Accounting for depreciation"

The content of this discussion paper is referred to in this survey in the section "Fixed assets".

Current Cost Accounting

The previous edition of the survey referred to the special meeting of the Institute of Chartered Accountants in England and Wales on July 1982, which debated a motion calling for the immediate withdrawal of SSAP 16. It also mentioned the subsequent statement by the Chairman of the Accounting Standards Committee, which confirmed that the standard remained in force, and the new constitution and new terms of reference of the ASC's Inflation Accounting Sub-Committee.

In April 1983, the ASC issued a statement which reiterated the fact that SSAP 16 remained in force and referred to an annexed interim report by the CCA Monitoring Working Party, set up to investigate the implementation of SSAP 16 on the ASC's behalf. The statement also referred to research projects and surveys being individually sponsored or conducted by the ASC's member bodies. The content of the ASC statement and the working party's interim report is described in more detail in the section "Current cost accounting". The working party's final report was issued in September 1983; it states that its findings and recommendations do not differ substantially from those of the interim report.

A joint statement by The Stock Exchange and the ASC in December 1982 announced that the provision of current cost accounting information in interim reports would no longer be mandatory under The Stock Exchange's listing requirements.

It is understood that an exposure draft, setting out proposals for revisions to SSAP 16, will be issued in January 1984.

EXAMPLES

Examples 1 to 5 illustrate different presentations found amongst companies adopting the new requirements of Schedule 8 to the Companies Act 1948. These presentations were highlighted above in sections 2(a) and 2(b) of the "Companies Act 1981" sub-section. Example 1 presents the vertical "Operational" profit and loss account format (Format 1) and Example 2 presents the vertical "Type of expenditure" format (Format 2). The only horizontal balance sheet (Format 2) format is presented as Example 3. Of the vertical balance sheets, Example 4 illustrates those who drew a total immediately before "Capital and reserves" (Heading K) and Example 5 illustrates those who drew a total immediately after "Total assets less current liabilities" (Heading G).

Example 1
British Sugar plc and Subsidiaries   *26 September 1982*
Consolidated Statement of profit and loss:

Prepared on the Current Cost Basis of Accounting

Notes		1982 £000	£000	1981 £000	£000
. .	**Turnover**		**523,742**		488,200
	Cost of sales		**416,821**		388,836
	Gross profit		**106,921**		99,364
	Distribution costs	**34,126**		35,360	
	Administrative expenses	**16,031**		15,093	
. .	Other operating expenses (net)	**7,885**		6,085	
			58,042		56,538
	Operating profit		**48,879**		42,826
. .	Investment income		**(2,278)**		—
	Profit before interest payable		**51,157**		42,826
	Interest on term loans	**6,888**		7,064	
	Gearing adjustment	**(3,175)**		(2,174)	
			3,713		4,890
. .	**Profit on ordinary activities before taxation**		**47,444**		37,936
. .	Taxation		**2,095**		6,477
	Profit on ordinary activities after taxation		**45,349**		31,459
. .	**Earnings per share**		**75.6 pence**		52.4 pence
	Utilisation of profit				
	Profit on ordinary activities after taxation		**45,349**		31,459
. .	Extraordinary items less taxation		**(31)**		13,717
	Profit for the financial year		**45,380**		17,742
. .	Dividends		**34,444**		15,000
. .	**Retained profit**		**10,936**		2,742

9

Example 2
Amalgamated Metal Corporation PLC *31 December 1982*
Consolidated profit and loss account:

	Notes	The Group 1982 £000	1981 £000
Turnover		1,637,970	1,410,602
Change in stocks of finished goods and work in progress		(8,440)	6,152
Own work capitalised		166	271
Other operating income		1,385	703
Total operating income		1,631,081	1,417,728
Raw materials and consumables		(1,586,155)	(1,372,458)
Other external charges		(5,700)	(6,437)
Staff costs – wages and salaries		(14,976)	(13,509)
– social security costs		(841)	(819)
– other pension costs		(1,461)	(1,139)
Depreciation and amounts written off tangible assets – normal depreciation		(1,656)	(1,557)
Other operating charges		(15,073)	(14,664)
Total operating costs	..	(1,625,862)	(1,410,583)
Operating profit		5,219	7,145
Share of profits less losses of related companies		152	54
Income from investments	..	1,961	1,341
Interest income		2,145	2,335
Profit before interest paid		9,477	10,875
Interest paid on borrowings repayable within five years		4,132	4,149
Profit on ordinary activities before taxation		5,345	6,726
Tax on profit on ordinary activities	..	2,252	3,796
Profit on ordinary activities after taxation		3,093	2,930
Minority interests		1,283	1,411
Profit before extraordinary items		1,810	1,519
27·0p per ordinary share (1981: 22·4p)	..		
Extraordinary items	..	280	(500)
Profit for the financial year attributable to shareholders		2,090	1,019
31·4p per ordinary share (1981: 14·4p)	..		
Dividends	..	114	240
Retained profit for the financial year		1,976	779

Example 3

Amalgamated Metal Corporation PLC　　31 December 1982

Balance sheet assets:

	Notes	The Company 1982 £000	1981 £000	The Group 1982 £000	1981 £000
Fixed assets					
Tangible assets	:	734	431	9,596	9,568
Shares in Group companies	:	14,513	19,568	—	—
Loans to Group companies	:	13,360	10,517	—	—
Shares in related companies	:	—	—	1,331	1,306
Other investments other than loans	:	—	—	4,924	4,556
		28,607	30,516	15,851	15,430
Current assets					
Stocks					
Raw materials and consumables		9	21	7,129	6,063
Work in progress		—	—	7,043	16,007
Finished goods		—	—	2,556	2,032
Goods for resale		6,864	3,773	35,176	31,978
Debtors					
Trade debtors	:	11,628	4,010	47,054	35,096
Advance payments against merchandise		12,098	6,032	49,778	17,349
Amounts owed by holding company and fellow subsidiaries		28	578	108	1,176
Amounts owned by subsidiaries		7,823	602	—	—
Amounts owned by related companies		27	—	27	150
Advance corporation tax recoverable		143	143	—	—
Taxation receivable		3,598	3,604	—	71
Other debtors		609	—	7,245	1,758
Prepayments and accrued income		147	—	570	591
Cash at bank and in hand	:	815	17	4,981	4,674
		43,789	18,780	161,667	116,945
		72,396	49,296	177,518	132,375

Balance sheet liabilities:

	Notes	The Company 1982 £000	1981 £000	The Group 1982 £000	1981 £000
Capital and reserves					
Called up share capital	:	8,591	8,591	8,591	8,591
Share premium account	:	1,265	1,265	1,265	1,265
Revaluation reserve	:	—	—	706	667
Profit and loss account	:	12,117	10,983	29,008	25,060
Shareholders' funds		21,973	20,839	39,570	35,583
Minority interests		—	—	8,563	7,404
		21,973	20,839	48,133	42,987
Provisions for liabilities and charges					
Pensions and similar obligations	:	—	—	383	292
Deferred taxation	:	89	100	638	680
Other provisions	:	—	—	684	1,193
		89	100	1,705	2,165
Creditors payable within one year	:				
Bank loans and overdrafts		7,128	2,997	22,745	17,332
Payments received on account		8,035	5,766	43,511	12,504
Trade creditors		15,949	2,743	47,552	39,972
Amounts owed to holding and fellow subsidiaries		62	10	97	90
Amounts owed to subsidiaries		16,623	15,920	—	—
Amounts owed to related companies		490	—	490	24
Dividends due to minority interests		—	—	388	653
Dividends payable to shareholders		57	57	57	57
Corporation tax		—	—	4,007	6,012
Taxation and social security payable		71	72	352	264
Other creditors		592	234	6,686	5,034
Accruals and deferred income		1,327	558	1,795	5,281
		50,334	28,357	127,680	87,223
		72,396	49,296	177,518	132,375

Example 4
Allied-Lyons *5 March 1983*
Balance Sheets:

	Notes	Group 1983 £m	1982 £m	Parent company 1983 £m	1982 £m
Fixed assets					
Tangible assets	../..	**1,088.4**	1,021.3	**9.7**	9.7
Investments	../..	**97.0**	90.5	**581.9**	627.4
		1,185.4	1,111.8	**591.6**	637.1
Current assets					
Stocks	..	**434.2**	444.0	—	—
Debtors	..	**270.6**	268.8	**10.1**	8.8
Cash at bank and in hand		**47.0**	32.3	**14.2**	11.6
Creditors (amounts falling due within one year)					
Short-term borrowings	..	**(67.8)**	(77.8)	**(32.9)**	48.9)
Other	..	**(452.2)**	428.2)	**(48.0)**	(46.8)
Net current assets		**231.8**	239.1	**(56.6)**	(75.3)
Total assets less current liabilities		**1,417.2**	1,350.9	**535.0**	561.8
Creditors (amounts falling due after more than one year)					
Loan capital	..	**(363.9)**	(350.9)	**(210.7)**	(259.6)
Other	..	**(17.5)**	(13.6)	—	—
Provisions for liabilities and charges					
Provisions for retirement benefits	..	**(16.5)**	(19.1)	**(14.5)**	(17.0)
Deferred taxation	..	**2.9**	(4.9)	**0.9**	0.9
		1,022.2	962.4	**310.7**	286.1
Capital and reserves					
Called up share capital	..	**170.4**	167.7	**170.4**	167.7
Share premium account	..	**74.9**	68.7	**74.9**	68.7
Revaluation reserve	..	**389.6**	392.1	—	—
Capital reserve	..	**84.8**	86.3	**41.2**	39.8
Profit and loss account	..	**268.2**	217.2	**24.2**	9.9
		987.9	932.0	**310.7**	286.1
Minority interests					
Preference shareholders		**12.9**	12.1	—	—
Ordinary shareholders		**21.4**	18.3	—	—
		1,022.2	962.4	**310.7**	286.1

Example 5
Reed International PLC *3 April 1983*
Historical Cost Balance sheets:

	HCA Consolidated				HCA Parent			
	1983		1982		**1983**		1982	
	£m	**£m**	£m	£m	**£m**	**£m**	£m	£m
Fixed assets								
Intangible assets note ..	**97·9**		76·3		—		—	
Tangible assets note..	**429·4**		391·0		**12·5**		13·1	
Investments note ..	**19·6**		18·7		**823·7**		677·0	
		546·9		486·0		**836·2**		690·1
Current assets								
Stocks note ..	**227·0**		222·5		—		—	
Debtors note ..	**339·5**		314·1		**20·8**		14·6	
Deferred taxation note ..	**4·1**		7·7		**0·5**		1·0	
Cash at bank and in hand	**53·0**		101·3		**19·1**		44·4	
	623·6		645·6		**40·6**		60·0	
Creditors: Amounts falling due within 1 year note ..								
Loan capital	**15·8**		11·7		**13·0**		9·9	
Other	**329·6**		318·6		**55·2**		67·3	
	345·4		330·3		**68·2**		77·2	
Net current assets		**278·2**		315·3		**(27·8)**		(17·2)
Total assets less current liabilities		**825·1**		801·3		**808·4**		672·9
Creditors: Amounts falling due after more than 1 year note ..								
Loan capital	**174·5**		177·2		**111·6**		113·3	
Other	**25·9**		23·3		**303·5**		174·4	
		200·4		200·5		**415·1**		287·7
Provisions for liabilities and charges note ..		**24·2**		27·6		—		0·1
Outside shareholders' interests		**3·9**		4·2		—		—
Capital and reserves								
Called up share capital note ..	**122·1**		121·8		**122·1**		121·8	
Share premium account note ..	**147·4**		147·1		**147·4**		147·1	
Revaluation reserve note ..	**61·5**		67·1		—		—	
Retained profits note ..	**265·6**		233·0		**123·8**		116·2	
		596·6		569·0		**393·3**		385·1
Capital employed		**825·1**		801·3		**808·4**		672·9

13

FURTHER READING

Accounting Standards Committee, "Review of the standard setting process", ASC, 1983.
——————————, SSAP 9 – Stocks and work in progress, ASC, 1981.
——————————, SSAP 16 – Current cost accounting, ASC, 1980.
——————————, SSAP 20 – Foreign currency translation, ASC, 1983.
——————————, ED 28 – Accounting for Petroleum Revenue Tax, ASC, 1981.
——————————, ED 29 – Accounting for leases and hire purchase contracts, ASC, 1981.
——————————, ED 30 – Accounting for goodwill, ASC, 1982.
——————————, ED 31 – Accounting for acquisitions and mergers, ASC, 1982.
——————————, ED 32 – Disclosure of pension information in company accounts, ASC, 1983.
——————————, ED 33 – Accounting for deferred tax, ASC, 1983.
——————————, "A review of SSAP 6 – Extraordinary items and prior year adjustments", ASC, 1983.
——————————, "A review of SSAP 12 – Accounting for depreciation", ASC, 1983.
——————————, "Statement by the Accounting Standards Committee on SSAP 16 – Current cost accounting", ASC, 1983.
——————————, "SSAP 16: Current Cost Accounting – Report of the Monitoring Working Party", ASC, 1983.
Accounting Standards Committee and The Stock Exchange, joint statement, "Current cost accounting information in interim reports", ASC and The Stock Exchange, 1982.
Companies Act, 1981, HMSO, 1981.
Companies (Beneficial Interests) Act 1983, HMSO, 1983.
Companies (Accounts) Regulations 1982, HMSO, 1983.
Employment Act 1982, HMSO, 1982.
Seventh Council Directive on consolidated accounts, Council of the European Communities, 1983.
The Employment Act 1982 (Commencement) Order 1982, HMSO, 1982.

ASSOCIATED COMPANIES

R. A. Wyld

INTRODUCTION

During the 1960's it became common for companies to bring into their financial statements their share of the profits of trade investments rather than the dividends alone; this is often known as the "equity method". It had become clear that because of the growing practice of companies to conduct part of their businesses through other companies which were not subsidiaries, to account for the dividends alone gave misleading information regarding earnings.

For these reasons an accounting standard, SSAP 1 "Accounting for the results of associated companies", was issued which defined those companies ("associated companies") which should be accounted for in this way. The standard has twice been amended, the latest version being effective for financial statements relating to accounting periods starting on or after 1st January 1982.

Until 1981, there was no statutory recognition of the special nature of companies in which, although not subsidiaries, the investing company had a significant interest. The Companies Act 1981 recognises these companies which it calls "related companies".

This section explains the definition of associated and related companies and the appropriate accounting treatment for them.

REQUIREMENTS

Statutory requirements

The Companies Act 1981 recognises for the first time, the special nature of what are called "related companies". These are defined as bodies corporate (other than group companies) in which a company holds, on a long-term basis, an interest in voting equity capital for the purpose of securing a contribution to that company's own activities by the exercise of any control or influence arising from that interest. Where the interest represents 20% or more of the relevant nominal equity capital the criteria will be presumed to have been met.

This definition is broadly equivalent to the definition of associated companies given in SSAP 1 (see below).

Schedule 8 of the 1948 Companies Act (as amended) requires shares in related companies to be carried in the investing company's own balance sheet as fixed assets, at cost less provision for any permanent diminution in value. Alternatively they may be carried at market value at the date of the last valuation or at a value determined on any basis which appears to the directors to be appropriate in the circumstances of the company; but, in the latter case, the basis and the reasons for adopting it must be disclosed. If they have not been accounted for by the equity method of valuation then, if material, additional information regarding underlying share capital, reserves and profits is to be given in respect of each investment.

If all investments falling within the definition of related companies are accounted for as associated companies the term "related companies" does not have to be used as long as the notes make it clear that there are no other related companies.

Standard accounting practice

An associated company is now defined as being a company, not being a subsidiary, in which the interest of the investing group or company is effectively that of a partner in a consortium or joint venture or is for the long term and is substantial and, having regard to the disposition of the other shareholdings, the investing group or company is in a position to exercise a significant influence over the company in which the investment is made.

Where the interest of the investing group or company is not effectively that of a partner in a joint venture or consortium, guidance is given as to what constitutes "significant influence". In particular, a holding of 20% or more of the equity voting rights of a company requires the presumption of the ability to exercise such influence; and a holding of less than 20% requires the contrary presumption unless, in either case, it can clearly be demonstrated otherwise. Where the holding is less than 20% this demonstration should include a statement from the associated company that it accepts that the investing company is in a position to exercise significant influence over it.

Earnings from associated companies are to be accounted for by bringing into the consolidated accounts the investing company's share of profits or losses as follows:

(a) profits less losses before taxation;
(b) taxation;
(c) extraordinary items (in the context of the group); and
(d) net profit less losses retained by associated companies.

The share of other items, such as turnover and depreciation, should not be included in the consolidated accounts. However, if one or more associates are material then separate disclosure of their total turnover and total depreciation should be given.

The investing company's own financial statements will only account for dividends received and receivable.

Except where it is a wholly-owned subsidiary, an investing company which does not prepare consolidated financial statements should show the information required by either preparing a separate profit and loss account or by adding the information in supplementary form to its own profit and loss account in such a way that its share of the undistributed profits of the associate is not treated as realised.

The amount at which SSAP 1 requires associated companies to be shown in the investing company's own balance sheet is either cost (less amounts written off) or valuation.

In the consolidated balance sheet, the basis for stating the investment in associated companies is:

(a) share of net assets, other than goodwill, of the associate;
(b) share of goodwill in the associates own financial statements; and
(c) premiums (or discount) on acquisition of the associate not written off

(a) should be shown separately.

The investing group's share of aggregate net profits less losses retained by associated companies should be shown separately in the financial statements of the investing group.

The International Accounting Standard on consolidated financial statements (IAS 3) specifies that the equity method of accounting for investments in

16

associated companies should be used. The requirements accord very closely with those of the UK Standard.

Stock Exchange

The Stock Exchange Listing Agreement (paragraph 10(e)) requires the following particulars to be given for each company (not being a subsidiary) in which the group interest in the equity capital amounts to 20% or more.

(i) the principal country of operation;
(ii) issued share capital and loan capital (and reserves if the group's interest is not dealt with as an associated company); and
(iii) the attributable percentage of each class of loan capital.

ANALYSIS

Table 1   **Associated company treatment**

		1982–83			1981–82
	Large listed	Medium listed	Large unlisted	Total	Total
Number of companies	*100*	*150*	*50*	*300*	*300*
Treatment adopted by companies reporting equity holdings of between 20% and 50% in other companies:	%	%	%	%	%
As associated companies in all cases	62	50	24	50	54
As associated companies in some cases	27	13	10	17	18
	89	63	34	67	72
Not as associated companies in any case	4	7	12	7	8
	93	70	46	74	80
No holding of between 20% and 50%	7	30	54	26	20
	100	100	100	100	100

Note: The differences shown in this table, between the treatments adopted by the three categories of company, are not statistically significant.

This table shows the accounting treatment adopted by the companies in the survey who reported investments of between 20% and 50% of the equity shares of other companies. The majority of these companies did not give all the names of these associated companies but only those of the principal companies together with the percentage interest in each. Most companies who had such holdings accounted for them as associated companies. Of those who did not, some 60%

17

gave reasons (see Table 2 below) although most of these were reporting under the old standard which did not require such a disclosure. This is a requirement of the revised standard, unless disclosure would be harmful to the business, and it may reasonably be expected that compliance will approach 100% in future.

Table 2   **Reasons for not using associated company treatment**

	1982–83				1981–82
	Large listed	Medium listed	Large unlisted	Total	Total
Number of companies	31	31	11	73	81
Reasons given:	%	%	%	%	%
Amounts involved not material	35	13	36	26	34
Insufficient influence of the investing company	14	9	18	12	19
Other reasons	19	26	18	22	2
	68	48	72	60	55
Reasons not given	32	52	28	40	45
	100	100	100	100	100

Note: The differences shown in this table, between the three categories of company, are not statistically significant.

Table 3   **Disclosure of attributable results of associated companies**

	1982–83				1981–82
	Large listed	Medium listed	Large unlisted	Total	Total
Number of companies	89	94	17	200	217
Attributable profits before tax, tax charge and retained profits	% 64	% 54	% 59	% 59	% 77
Attributable profits before tax and tax charge	30	37	24	33	14
Other	6	9	17	8	9
	100	100	100	100	100

Note: The differences shown in this table, between the three categories of company, are not statistically significant.

The nature of the information provided by the companies which included attributable profits and losses of associated companies in the profit and loss account is summarised above in Table 3. As will be seen from the table, a substantial number of companies did not show separately the share of net profits less losses retained although in some cases it was possible to calculate this from other information given.

Table 4   **Associated companies in the consolidated balance sheet**

	Large listed	Medium listed	Large unlisted	Total	Total
		1982–83			*1981–82*
Number of companies	89	94	17	200	217
Measurement basis for investments:	%	%	%	%	%
Cost less amounts written off, plus share of post-acquisition retained profits and reserves	93	90	88	92	83
Cost or valuation	5	10	12	7	15
Not stated	2	—	—	1	2
	100	100	100	100	100
Disclosure of attributable retained profits and reserves:					
Separately shown	62	55	41	57	55
Not separately shown	38	45	59	43	44
No reserves/No information	—	—	—	—	1
	100	100	100	100	100

Note: The differences shown in this table, between the measurement and the disclosure practices of the three categories of company, are not statistically significant.

As can be seen from Table 4, almost all the companies used the basis laid down in SSAP 1 for the carrying value of associated companies in the balance sheet. The revised standard requires the goodwill element to be identified, either by showing separately the premium paid (or discount) on acquisition and the investing group's share of goodwill in the associates own accounts, or these two items combined. It appears, from the information given in the accounts that were subject to the new requirements, that most companies have written off goodwill on acquisition.

Table 5   **Definition of an associated company**

	Large listed	Medium listed	Large unlisted	Total
		1982–83		
Number of companies	93	105	23	221
	%	%	%	%
In accord with SSAP 1	38	34	22	34
Not in accord with SSAP 1	1	2	—	1
No definition given	61	64	78	65
	100	100	100	100

Note: The differences shown in this table, between the three categories of company, are not statistically significant.

19

SSAP 1 does not require a definition to be given. Nevertheless, of the companies which had equity holdings of between 20% and 50% in other companies, over a third gave a definition, usually in the accounting policies note. The definition given by three companies was not in accord with SSAP 1 in that no reference was made to the exercise of significant influence over the associate.

Conclusion

It will be noted from the tables that non-compliance with SSAP 1 is relatively common. For example, although the standard requires accumulated reserves to distinguish between profits retained by the group and profits retained by associated companies almost half the companies in the sample did not do so.

The explanatory foreword to the Statements of Standard Accounting Practice says that if there is a significant departure from accounting standards this should be disclosed and explained. The auditors are expected to ensure disclosure of significant departures and, to the extent that their concurrence is stated or implied, to justify them. This means that if no disclosure is made in the accounts the auditors must give the information in their report. There was only one example of the auditors doing this.

EXAMPLES

The example illustrates information given on the accounting treatment for associated companies. It is particularly interesting in the way it shows full details of the share of associates profits and combines this with the net asset carrying value on the balance sheet. The purist would fault the inclusion of associated company turnover in the turnover analysis on the profit and loss account but this is the only blemish on an otherwise well thought out presentation.

Example
Powell Duffryn Public Limited Company   *31 March 1983*
Group Profit and Loss Account:

For the year ended 31st March	Notes	**1983 £000**	1982 £000
Turnover			
Subsidiary companies		**507,389**	499,097
Associated companies – share of turnover	12	**88,413**	87,487
		595,802	586,584
Trading Profit			
Subsidiary companies	. .	**18,517**	17,250
Associated companies – share of profits	12	**1,985**	1,888
Group Trading Profit		**20,502**	19,138
Interest	. .	**7,560**	6,633
Profit before Taxation		**12,942**	12,505
Taxation	. .	**4,069**	2,496
Profit after Taxation		**8,873**	10,009
Extraordinary items	. .	**3,118**	488
Consolidated Net Profit attributable to Powell Duffryn plc		**5,755**	9,521
Dividends on preference shares		**60**	60
Profit attributable to Ordinary Shareholders		**5,695**	9,461
Dividends on ordinary shares:			
Interim 4·7p per share paid on 6 January 1983 (1982 4·7p)		**1,473**	1,473
Final proposed 9·55p per share (1982 9·55p)		**2,986**	2,986
		1,236	5,002
Profit Retained			
Powell Duffryn plc		**508**	58
Subsidiary companies		**108**	3,894
Associated companies		**620**	1,050
		1,236	5,002
Net earnings per ordinary share based on the weighted average number of shares in issue during the year of 31,278,000 (1982 31,259,000) and on profit before extraordinary items:			
net basis (after ACT written off)		**28·2p**	31·8p
Dividend – times covered		**2·0**	2·2

21

	Group 1983 £000	Parent Company 1983 £000	Subsidiary Companies 1983 £000	Associated Companies 1983 £000
8 Reserves				
Balance at 31 March 1982	88,793	27,083	53,556	8,154
Exchange adjustments	458	—	432	26
Profit retained	1,236	508	108	620
Goodwill on acquisitions of companies	439	—	207	232
(Deficit)/Surplus on revaluation of fixed assets	420	—	104	524
	89,628	27,591	53,993	8,044

	Group 1983 £000	1982 £000
12 Associated Companies		
Share of results of associated companies:		
Turnover	88,413	87,487
Profit before taxation	1,985	1,888
Taxation	476	359
Profit after taxation	1,509	1,529
Dividends	889	479
Retained profit	620	1,050
Movements on reserves	730	500
Share of undistributed profit at start of year	8,154	7,604
Share of undistributed profit since acquisition	8,044	8,154
Group share of net assets	11,443	10,931
Loans to associated companies (including parent company £412,000)	2,145	1,655
	13,588	12,586

The principal associated companies of the Group are listed
on pages . . and . .

FURTHER READING

Wild, K. *An Accountants Digest Guide to Accounting Standards – Accounting for Associated Companies*, Accountants Digest 126, The Institute of Chartered Accountants in England and Wales, 1982.

CURRENT COST ACCOUNTING

J. H. Plowdon and D. P. Tweedie

INTRODUCTION

Most listed and large unlisted companies are required to produce current cost accounts in accordance with SSAP 16 "Current Cost Accounting" as part of their annual financial report either in the form of main or supplementary statements. When the standard was introduced in 1980, the Accounting Standards Committee stated that there would be a "trial period" of three years during which no changes would be made to SSAP 16 to enable companies to become accustomed to the new requirements, and that a review would be undertaken at the end of this period. Since its introduction, however, inflation has steadily fallen and interest in inflation accounting seems to have declined. This was probably exacerbated by the publication of the government's Green Paper (Cmnd. 8456, 1982) which indicated that it was unlikely that corporation tax would be based on current cost accounts. This view was hardly surprising given the announcement in 1980 of stock relief based on a general stock index, the present subjective measurement bases of CCA and the nature of existing reliefs.

At the time of writing, the promised review is under way and a considerable amount of debate and research work is currently being undertaken on the subject. A "CCA Monitoring Working Party" formed by the Accounting Standards Committee has recently published an interim report ("The Neville Report") based on the outcome of consultative meetings held with a wide range of users, preparers and auditors of current cost accounts. The Accounting Standards Committee, having considered the report, has published (see, for example, *The Accountant's Magazine*, May 1983, page 169 and pages 187–188) three points for general discussion which could possibly give an insight into the direction in which the whole debate is heading:

"1) Where a company is materially affected by changing prices, pure HC accounts do not give a true and fair view. For this reason, a company's main accounts should reflect the effect of changing prices either in the arithmetic of the profit and loss account and balance sheet or in the notes to the accounts. It is implicit in this that there should be only one set of accounts.

2) The standard should prescribe more than one method of accounting for the effects of changing prices, so that companies can employ a method which is appropriate to their particular circumstances and activities.

3) The standard should apply to all accounts intended to give a true and fair view, subject to a cost-benefit test, to be applied by ASC in preparing its proposals for the standard, which recognises the differing requirements of shareholders and other users for information."

It appears, from both The Neville Report and the 14812 votes (48%) [out of 30557] cast against SSAP 16 at the Special General Meeting of the ICAEW in July 1982, that the standard has become unpopular and that a new standard, expected in early 1985, might be significantly different from the present one. Consequently, we have modified the approach normally taken in the survey and have concentrated less on the presentation of current cost accounts than on the problems companies faced in implementing the standard. By examining the

23

reasons for non-compliance, the complaints about the standard and any additional voluntary disclosures, we hope to obtain an insight into the possible future direction for inflation accounting in the UK. Firstly, however, what are companies currently expected to produce?

REQUIREMENTS

Statutory requirements

For the period covered by this survey, the statutory requirements in connection with current cost accounts were not especially onerous, although the requirements of the Companies Act 1981 have now, for the first time, enshrined some current cost accounting principles in statute.

Section 149 of the Companies Act 1948 requires every balance sheet and profit and loss account to show a "true and fair" view. This can be satisfied by the production of either historical cost accounts or current cost accounts. Schedule 1 to the Companies Act 1981 (now Schedule 8 to the 1948 Act) outlines accounting rules in more detail and specifically permits the use of alternative (to historical cost) accounting rules in the main financial statements. Under these rules, companies are, for example, permitted to include tangible fixed assets at valuation or at their current cost and certain current assets (including stocks) at current cost but, when these bases are used, the historical cost amounts (or differences therefrom) for these assets, excluding stocks, have to be disclosed.

Fortunately, the alternative rules are worded in general terms which allow considerable scope for future developments in current cost valuation methods. Problems may well arise for the standard-setters, however, from the provision (in para 12 of the new Schedule 8) that only realised profits may be included in the profit and loss account. This rule, unless swept aside by the true and fair override, could restrict the future development of inflation accounting in the UK, effectively blocking, in the statutory accounts, the internationally popular "real" terms solution to the problem of accounting for price-level changes. In broad terms, a "real" terms system combines the revaluation of individual assets by reference to specific price changes with a general index adjustment of equity capital.

Standard accounting practice

SSAP 16 (para 46) applies to all annual financial statements intended to give a true and fair view, except financial statements of:

    (a) unlisted companies which satisfy at least two of the following three criteria:
        (i)   turnover less than £5,000,000 per annum;
        (ii) balance sheet total (fixed assets, investments and current assets) at the beginning of the period less than £2,500,000;
        (iii) average number of employees in the United Kingdom or in the Republic of Ireland less than 250.
    (b) wholly owned subsidiaries where the parent is registered in the United Kingdom or in the Republic of Ireland (unless the parent is exempted under (c) and (d) below, in which case current cost information for subsidiaries not themselves exempted is required);

(c) entities whose long term primary financial objective is other than to achieve an operating profit (charities, building societies etc.);

(d) (i) authorised insurers;

    (ii) property investment and dealing entities (excluding companies which hold group properties for companies to whom SSAP 16 applies);

    (iii) investment trust companies, unit trusts and similar long term investment entities.

Those companies which fall within the scope of SSAP 16 are required (paras 47–48) to produce current cost accounts which contain a profit and loss account, balance sheet and appropriate notes, either as their main or supplementary statements. Only three companies in the survey were exempt from the requirements of the standard.

Profit and loss account

The main disclosure requirements for the profit and loss account, together with associated notes, (paras 55–56) are *inter alia*: a reconciliation between the current cost operating profit and the historical cost profit showing the respective amounts for depreciation, cost of sales and monetary working capital adjustments; a gearing adjustment; and the current cost profit after tax attributable to shareholders. Listed companies should also show the current cost earnings per share (para 59).

Balance sheet

The balance sheet and associated notes should disclose (para 57) *inter alia*: the assets of the entity on the current cost basis; totals of net operating assets and net borrowings together with their main elements; a summary of the fixed asset accounts; and movements on reserves.

Notes

There is a specific requirement (para 58) for notes to the current cost accounts to describe the bases and methods adopted in preparing the accounts, with particular attention being given to:

(i) the value to the business of fixed assets and stocks and the current cost adjustments relating thereto;

(ii) the monetary working capital and gearing adjustments;

(iii) the basis of translating foreign currencies and dealing with translation differences arising;

(iv) corresponding amounts; and

(v) other material adjustments to the historical cost information.

The explanatory note to the standard (paras 34–37) also outlines the additional voluntary disclosures which companies should consider providing in their accounts. These include: information reflecting a gearing adjustment calculated on a different basis from that provided in the standard (e.g. an adjustment based on all holding gains as proposed in the New Zealand standard), where this is more appropriate to the circumstances of the company; and a statement of the change in shareholders' equity interest after allowing for the change in the general purchasing power of money – for those companies which prefer a "real" terms solution to the problem of accounting for price level changes.

Both of these voluntary disclosures, subjects of controversy when SSAP 16 was being drafted, represent ways by which changes could be made to SSAP 16. They have, therefore, specifically been incorporated in our analysis to ascertain whether any of the companies in our survey have indicated, by means of these disclosures, the way in which they might like the inflation accounting debate to develop.

ANALYSIS

Introduction

At a time when the ASC is considering the future of inflation accounting in the United Kingdom, our aim in this analysis is to consider the effect on historical cost profit of current cost adjustments; to obtain insights into the type of company which fails to comply with SSAP 16; to examine problems encountered in applying the standard; to analyse the bases adopted for the purposes of current cost accounts; and finally, as mentioned above, to discover whether any companies appeared to support other systems of accounting for price level changes by providing additional information.

Accordingly, this section considers initially (Tables 1 to 4) the impact of the standard on those companies which complied with its provisions. We then examine those companies which did not provide SSAP 16 information (Tables 5 to 8), before analysing the criticisms made and problems encountered by the companies complying with SSAP 16 (Tables 9 to 11). Tables 12 to 14 outline the bases adopted by companies in producing current cost information.

Two caveats should be observed when interpreting the following data. Firstly, the sample of 300 companies included in this survey has changed from that used in previous years. As a result of this, and the change in emphasis of this year's chapter, comparative figures are considerably less meaningful than they have been in previous surveys. Secondly, it must be remembered that the companies surveyed may not be representative of all the companies within the categories or industries mentioned in this chapter. The detailed analysis should therefore be interpreted with caution.

The impact of current cost adjustments on historical cost profit before taxation

Apart from presenting the effect of the current cost adjustments in Tables 1 to 4 below, we also wished to test whether or not those companies upon which SSAP 16 had a greater impact would be more likely to complain about the standard than companies upon whom the impact was less. Consequently, we used the information derived in the following four tables to test this, the results of which are reported after Table 10.

The information in Tables 1 to 4 is presented in terms of each category of company without excluding those companies which did not provide SSAP 16 accounts. Our aim is to show the impact of the adjustments on the *total* survey sample. Additionally, we believe that the very small number of unlisted companies complying with the provisions of SSAP 16 could give a misleading impression if the tables were to be constructed by excluding companies which

26

did not provide SSAP 16 accounts. We do however discuss briefly in the text the effect of the adjustments on each category of company computed on this alternative basis. (Readers wishing to ascertain the overall effect of the adjustments on each category of company as a proportion of those companies complying with SSAP 16, can, of course, recompute, ignoring the last line of the tables.)

Table 1   **Impact of the depreciation adjustment**

| | 1982–83 | | | |
	Large listed	Medium listed	Large unlisted	Total
Number of companies	100	150	50	300
	%	%	%	%
Companies which made an HC loss	6	15	2	10
Adjustment as a % of HC profit before taxation:				
0 – 10%	8	21	12	15
11 – 20%	28	29	4	24
21 – 30%	23	10	6	14
>30%	24	15	8	17
No SSAP 16 accounts	11	10	68	20
	100	100	100	100

The proportions of large listed, medium listed and large unlisted companies providing SSAP 16 accounts, and reporting a depreciation adjustment of more than 20% were 53%, 28% and 44% respectively. The impact of the depreciation adjustment on the medium listed companies is, therefore, considerably lower than on the other two categories. This result, when tested statistically, was found to be significant.

The net effect of the cost of sales and monetary working capital adjustments (henceforth COSA and MWCA respectively) on historical cost profit, as can be seen from Table 2 below, is generally less than that of the depreciation adjustment but is still considerable in absolute terms.

Table 2   **Impact of the cost of sales plus monetary working capital adjustments**

	1982–83			
	Large listed	*Medium listed*	*Large unlisted*	*Total*
Number of companies	*100*	*150*	*50*	*300*
	%	%	%	%
Companies which made an HC loss	6	15	2	10
Adjustment as a % of HC profit before taxation:				
0 – 10%	22	27	10	23
11 – 20%	32	19	10	22
21 – 30%	12	14	4	11
>30%	17	15	6	14
No SSAP 16 accounts	11	10	68	20
	100	100	100	100

Excluding those companies which failed to provide SSAP 16 accounts, the proportion of large listed, medium listed and large unlisted companies which reported a COSA plus MWCA adjustment in excess of 20% was 32% in each case.

Table 3   **Impact of the gearing adjustment**

	1982–83			
	Large listed	*Medium listed*	*Large unlisted*	*Total*
Number of companies	*100*	*150*	*50*	*300*
	%	%	%	%
Companies which made an HC loss	6	15	2	10
Adjustment as a % of HC profit before taxation:				
0 – 5%	27	40	18	32
6 – 10%	18	17	6	15
11 – 20%	21	8	2	11
21 – 30%	14	4	2	7
>30%	3	6	2	5
No SSAP 16 accounts	11	10	68	20
	100	100	100	100

Since the gearing adjustment, by definition, is a proportion of the depreciation, cost of sales and monetary working capital adjustments, its impact on historical cost profit before taxation will not be as material as the combination of the other adjustments and this is supported by the above results. Furthermore, a comparison by category of the proportion of companies which reported a gearing adjustment above 5% of HC profit before taxation shows that the benefit of the adjustment is greater for the large listed companies (63%) than for the medium listed (39%) and large unlisted (37%) companies. When the impact of the adjustment on the large listed companies was compared with that on the other two categories the test was statistically significant.

There are two main factors contributing to this result: firstly the impact of the other current cost adjustments tended to be greater (see Tables 1 and 2) for the large listed companies than the others; and secondly, the financial gearing of the large listed companies was higher than that of the other companies.

Table 4 **Impact of the net CCA adjustments**

| | 1982–83 | | | |
	Large listed	Medium listed	Large unlisted	Total
Number of companies	100	150	50	300
	=	=	=	=
	%	%	%	%
Companies which made an HC loss	6	15	2	10
Adjustment as a % of HC profit before taxation:				
0 – 10%	5	16	4	10
11 – 20%	18	17	6	15
21 – 30%	20	15	4	15
>30%	40	27	16	30
No SSAP 16 accounts	11	10	68	20
	100	100	100	100

As a proportion of historical cost profit, the overall impact of current cost adjustments was considerable even in a period of falling inflation, Table 4 revealing that 30% of all companies had net adjustments in excess of 30% of historical cost profit before taxation. For the population of companies providing SSAP 16 accounts, the impact of current cost adjustments greater than 20% of historical cost profit is lowest (47%) on the medium listed companies (67% for large listed companies and 63% for large unlisted companies). A statistical comparison of the results for the medium listed companies with the combined results of the other categories proved to be significant.

Failure to provide current cost statements

Having determined the impact of SSAP 16 on the different categories of companies, the next part of the analysis was to examine those companies which did not provide current cost accounts.

Table 5　　　　　　　　　　**Current cost statements provided**

	Large listed	Medium listed	Large unlisted	Total	Total
		1982–83			*1981–82*
Number of companies	*100*	*150*	*50*	*300*	*300*
	%	%	%	%	%
CC statements provided:					
SSAP 16 – audited	85	86	32	77	
– unaudited	4	4	–	3	
	89	90	32	80	94
CC statements provided:					
Other – audited	1	—	2	1	1
CC statements not provided:					
Omission explained by directors	8	9	22	11	4
Omission noted but not explained by directors	–	–	2	1	–
Not mentioned by directors	–	1	40	6	1
	8	10	64	18	5
CC statements not required ...	2	—	2	1	—
	100	100	100	100	100

A comparison of this year's large listed companies with the total 1981–82 sample (possibly the most meaningful comparison) indicates an increase in non-compliance from 5% to 8%. It is interesting to note that all but one of the listed companies which did not comply with SSAP 16 provided reasons for not doing so but a considerable proportion of the large unlisted companies (40%) failed even to note this matter in their financial statements. A statistical comparison by category of company, comparing those that provided SSAP 16 accounts with those that failed to comply, produced a significant result. This is not surprising given the very high proportion (64%) of large unlisted companies which failed to provide current cost statements.

Due to the recession experienced in the United Kingdom many companies have been reporting considerably reduced profits in historical cost terms. Furthermore, as we have seen, current cost adjustments during inflationary conditions can reduce historical cost profits considerably. In order to establish whether there is any correlation between the companies which failed to comply with SSAP 16 and a low level of profitability, these two factors were specifically examined and we show the results in Table 6 below. In each case, profitability has been computed with reference to the return (historical cost profit before taxation) on net assets.

Table 6   Return on net assets for companies which did not provide SSAP 16 statements

| | Large listed | | Medium listed | | Large unlisted | | Total | |
| | *1982–83* | | | | | | | |
	No SSAP16 accounts	*Total survey sample*	*No SSAP16 accounts*	*Total survey sample*	*No SSAP16 accounts*	*Total survey sample*	*No SSAP16 accounts*	*Total survey sample*
Number of companies	8	100	15	150	32	50	55	300
	%	%	%	%	%	%	%	%
Companies which made an HC loss	25	8	33	18	13	10	20	13
HC profit as a % return on net assets:								
0– 5%	12	5	13	5	3	8	7	6
6–10%	12	22	7	11	6	8	7	14
11–20%	39	38	40	40	50	42	46	40
>20%	12	27	7	26	28	32	20	27
	100	100	100	100	100	100	100	100

Table 6 shows that the companies which did not produce SSAP 16 statements are not restricted only to those who have achieved a low level of profitability during the year, a large proportion of unlisted companies failed to comply with SSAP 16 even though their return on net assets was generally better than that of the listed companies.

Considering the listed companies separately, there appears to be a tendency for the companies which report generally lower returns, when compared to the returns of the other listed companies in the survey, to fail to comply with SSAP 16. This was tested statistically by combining the large and medium listed companies and comparing the historical cost return of the listed companies which produced SSAP 16 accounts with the historical cost return of the listed companies which did not. The test was undertaken employing the return on net assets of 5% as the cut-off point for high/low profitability and the result was statistically significant. It would seem that listed companies are more likely not to comply with SSAP 16 when their historical cost profitability is low.

We also examined the principal activities of the companies which did not produce current cost accounts in an attempt to discover whether companies in particular industries were more likely than companies in other industries to fail to comply with SSAP 16. To avoid arbitrary categorisation we subdivided the population into twelve major industry classes. Table 7 shows the results as applicable to the survey sample.

31

Table 7   **Industry classification of companies which did not provide SSAP 16 statements**

	1982–83 *Total Survey*	
	No SSAP 16 accounts %	*Total survey sample n*
Industrial (General)......................	9	80
Building/Property	31	35
Engineering	16	31
Food	30	30
Motors/Aircraft	23	22
Stores.................................	14	21
Newspapers.............................	29	14
Oil/Gas	38	8
Overseas	50	6
Shipping	60	5
Financial	20	5
Tobacco................................	25	4

The "problem" industries appear to be building/property, food, newspapers, oil/gas and shipping, although the companies which did not provide SSAP 16 statements covered a wide range of industries.

Table 8   **Analysis of explanations given by directors when SSAP 16 statements not provided**

	1982–83			
	Large listed n	*Medium listed n*	*Large unlisted n*	*Total n*
Not relevant to industry	4	4	5	13
Costs outweigh benefits	1	4	3	8
No practical benefit to shareholders or management	1	3	1	5
Doubtful about methodology/subjectivity	—	3	1	4
No indices available in countries where significant activities occur	—	4	—	4
Other reasons	3	3	2	8
	9	21	12	42

Table 8 above analyses in detail the reasons given by chairmen or directors for not complying with SSAP 16. In a number of instances, more than one comment was made by 33 companies to which this analysis applies.

The most common comment was that the present standard was inappropriate to particular industries. The companies involved spanned seven industries with the food industry accounting for six of the thirteen companies involved. The other companies represented oil/gas (3), building/property (2), shipping (1) and one company whose interests were "wide" on both a geographical and industrial basis. It is interesting to note that two of the four large listed companies, while stating that SSAP 16 was not appropriate to their industry, provided additional information relating to fixed assets and a depreciation adjustment on a current cost basis.

The second and third items in Table 8 clearly are subjective statements which, in many cases, cannot be substantiated. Of the eight comments made that the costs of obtaining current cost information outweighs its benefits, three companies indicated that their operations were particularly complex. The other comments were of a more general nature. Of the five companies commenting that current cost accounts did not provide practical benefit to shareholders or management, two reported significant historical cost losses. The other comments, together with those about the methods/subjectivity of SSAP 16, were of a more general nature.

It would appear that the Accounting Standards Committee has given some attention to these problems since it has suggested that the new standard may be "subject to a cost-benefit test" and should prescribe more than one method to enable companies to select the one most appropriate to their circumstances. The Accounting Standards Committee presumably hopes that, as a result, the new standard will achieve wider acceptance than the present one.

Problems of companies complying with the standard

1 Criticisms made

Criticisms of, or comments on, SSAP 16 were made by chairmen or directors whose companies complied with the standard. These are summarised in Table 9 below. In some cases companies made more than one criticism or comment, in which case each was included separately in the following table. The total number of companies making criticisms of SSAP 16 was 24 while those making comments about the standard totalled 5.

Table 9   Criticism/comments on SSAP 16 where CCA statements provided

	Large listed n	Medium listed n	Large unlisted n	Total n
1982–83				
Criticisms:				
Criticism of SSAP 16 in general terms				
– audited	2	5	–	7
– unaudited	4	6	–	10
Need for CCA noted but not in form of				
SSAP 16......................	1	3	–	4
Criticism of individual adjustments	2	3	–	5
	9	17	–	26
Comments:				
Comments on future of CCA/SSAP 16 ..	4	1	–	5
Other comments	2	–	–	2
	15	18	–	33

While undertaking our examination of companies making general criticisms of SSAP 16, all of which were listed companies, we frequently noted that directors had asked their auditors not to audit the current cost accounts and we therefore included all the companies in the survey with unaudited current cost accounts in this category.

The effect of the net current cost adjustments on the historical cost profit before taxation of the 24 companies was as shown in Table 10 below.

Table 10   Effect of net CCA adjustments on historical cost profit before taxation for companies making criticisms of SSAP 16

	Large listed	Medium listed	Large unlisted	Total
1982–83				
Number of companies	9	15	Nil	24
	%	%	%	%
Companies which made an HC loss	11	20	–	17
Adjustment as a % of HC profit:				
0 – 10%	–	13	–	8
11 – 20%	–	7	–	4
21 – 30%	11	13	–	13
>30%............................	78	47	–	58
	100	100	–	100

It is interesting to compare the above results with those for the total survey sample. The percentage of listed companies in the total survey sample reporting current cost adjustments greater than 20% of historical cost profit before taxation was 55%, the comparable figure for only those companies making criticisms of SSAP 16 being 71%. A statistical examination of this result proved not to be significant.

We also noted that 14 of the 24 companies making criticisms of SSAP 16 achieved a historical cost rate of return (computed on the same basis as discussed in Table 6) of less than 10% (four made losses). This may provide some evidence as to why the impact of the current cost adjustments is appreciably higher for this sample when compared with the impact on all the listed companies in the survey. It would appear that low profits may provoke criticism of the standard or non-compliance with its provisions.

2 Problems encountered in applying SSAP 16

It is generally accepted that, due to the recession in the economy over the last few years, the practical application of SSAP 16 principles can cause problems particularly in determining the valuation of fixed assets, especially when assets are to be valued at recoverable amount. Few companies, however, (circa 10% of those complying fully with the standard) mentioned any practical difficulties and only five specifically noted problems with fixed asset valuation (Table 11). Unless few problems were experienced in applying the standard, it would appear that the ASC, as it seeks to improve upon SSAP 16, is receiving little guidance from disclosure in company accounts on the difficulties of implementing SSAP 16.

Table 11   **Problems encountered in applying SSAP 16**

| | 1982–83 | | | |
	Large listed	Medium listed	Large unlisted	Total
Obtaining current cost information from associates	4	12	—	16
Identifying replacement cost of fixed assets	—	5	—	5
Suitable indices not available	1	1	—	2
Other	1	1	—	2
	6	19	—	25

Note: The differences shown in this table, between the problems encountered by the three categories of company, are not statistically significant.

Two of the 16 companies noting problems in obtaining current cost information from associates estimated the appropriate adjustments, the historical cost figures being used by the other companies. Furthermore, in addition to these 16, four other companies made no comment but simply "excluded" associates from adjustment in their current cost accounts.

35

Conclusions

Before continuing with an examination of the bases adopted by companies for assessing current cost valuations and adjustments, we summarise briefly the main results discussed in the analysis section so far.

1 Even during a period of reducing inflation, the overall impact of current cost adjustments as a percentage of historical cost profit was considerable (Table 4), the impact shown statistically to be significantly less on the medium listed companies than on the other two groups.

2 8% of large listed companies, 10% of medium listed companies and 64% of unlisted companies failed to provide current cost statements (Table 5); the difference between the categories of company being statistically significant. Listed companies generally provided reasons for non-compliance but two thirds of the unlisted companies which failed to comply with SSAP 16 did not refer to this matter in their financial statements.

3 The companies which did not provide SSAP 16 statements covered a wide range of activities although building/property, food, newspapers, oil/gas and shipping companies were particularly prominent among those which failed to comply with the standard (Table 7).

4 For listed companies in the survey, there is a statistically significant relationship between a low level of historical cost profitability and failure to comply with SSAP 16 (Table 6).

5 The companies which criticised SSAP 16, but nevertheless complied with the requirements of the standard, generally achieved a low level of profitability and the impact of the current cost adjustments as a proportion of their historical cost profits was high (Table 10).

6 A majority of the problems which were encountered in applying SSAP 16 and which were noted by companies in their financial statements, related to difficulties in obtaining current cost information from associates (Table 11). Only five comments specifically related to the valuation of fixed assets on a current cost basis.

Having assessed the reasons given for non-compliance with SSAP 16 and the criticisms made of the standard, we now turn to the mechanics of implementing the policies adopted in preparing the current cost accounts.

Bases adopted for assessing current cost valuations and adjustments

1 Fixed assets

For the purposes of this examination, fixed assets were divided into three categories, investment properties, non-investment properties and other fixed assets. Investment properties did not result in divergent approaches to valuation – a direct valuation method with no depreciation (SSAP 19 "Accounting for investment properties") being employed in all cases where relevant. The non-investment properties displayed the widest diversity of methods ranging from direct valuation (91 companies – 38% of those to whom it applied) to a mixture of index based and direct valuation methods (58 companies – 24%). A majority of companies (88%) applied indices to historical cost amounts for other fixed assets, the remainder employing some direct valuation as well as indices.

2 Cost of sales and monetary working capital adjustments

A variety of methods was employed by companies in the preparation of the COSA and MWCA and these are summarised in the following two tables.

Table 12 **Bases for assessing the cost of sales adjustment**

| | 1982–83 | | | |
	Large listed	Medium listed	Large unlisted	Total
Number of companies	*100*	*150*	*50*	*300*
	%	%	%	%
Index based:				
– specific external	4	21	4	12
– specific internal	7	4	–	5
– not specified or combination of types	38	40	18	36
	49	65	22	53
Mixture of index based and direct valuation	13	5	2	7
Direct valuation	8	5	–	5
No details provided	16	10	2	10
No SSAP 16 accounts or no adjustment	14	15	74	25
	100	100	100	100

Table 13 **Bases for assessing the monetary working capital adjustment**

| | 1982–83 | | | |
	Large listed	Medium listed	Large unlisted	Total
Number of companies	*100*	*150*	*50*	*300*
	%	%	%	%
Index based:				
– general	1	2	2	2
– specific external	8	23	10	16
– specific internal	4	4	–	3
– not specified or combination of types	49	41	16	39
	62	70	28	60
Mixture of index based and direct valuation	6	1	–	3
Based upon actual movements in prices of sales and purchases	1	1	–	1
No details provided	20	15	4	15
No SSAP 16 accounts or no adjustment	11	13	68	21
	100	100	100	100

As can be seen from Tables 12 and 13 above, the most popular method for computing COSA and MWCA was by the application of indices (internal and external) to the historical cost amounts. For those companies to which these adjustments were applicable (and which provided sufficient information to ascertain the method used) only approximately 18% included some form of direct valuation to assess COSA.

Table 14   Definition of monetary working capital adjustment

	1982–83			
	Large listed	*Medium listed*	*Large unlisted*	*Total*
Number of companies	*100*	*150*	*50*	*300*
	%	%	%	%
Debtors less creditors..................	12	13	6	11
Trade debtors less trade creditors........	28	20	6	20
Debtors, creditors cash, short term borrowings and investments	6	5	2	5
Debtors, creditors fluctuating cash, short term borrowings and investments	11	6	–	7
Debtors, creditors and other net current assets regarded as forming part of MWC	16	12	8	13
Insufficient details given to identify components	16	32	10	23
No SSAP 16 accounts or no adjustments	11	12	68	21
	100	100	100	100

At first sight it would seem from Table 14 that many differing definitions of monetary working capital are being adopted and that a large proportion of companies (31%) have adopted a simple definition based solely on debtors less creditors. On the other hand, however, the differences may be indicative of the varying levels of disclosure between companies and be more a sign of inattention to the detail of disclosure. It is, consequently, difficult to judge whether or not vastly differing definitions of monetary working capital are being adopted.

3 Gearing adjustment

The gearing adjustment received a considerable amount of criticism from many sources during the debate leading up to the publication of SSAP 16. It is surprising, therefore, that only one company did not provide a gearing adjustment and only four others, whilst complying with the SSAP 16 method of computation, provided details of a gearing adjustment computed on an alternative basis. In two of these four cases the alternative adjustment was computed by applying an index reflecting the general rate of inflation to net monetary items not included in the MWCA and in the other instances adjustments were made to the recommended SSAP 16 method by:

1 reflecting the *total* holding gains less losses on assets effectively financed by borrowings and also incorporating exchange gains/losses on the non-sterling part of these net borrowings;
2 calculating the gearing adjustment by relating specific liabilities to specific assets.

Hence, there is little evidence in company accounts of criticism of the SSAP 16 gearing adjustment or of significant interest in developing a new form of gearing adjustment to reflect the gain on long term borrowings during a period of inflation.

General

Of the 229 companies which declared a dividend and produced current cost accounts, 87 (38%) declared a dividend in excess of current cost earnings. Of these 87 companies, 23 reported current cost losses. Clearly, the existence of current cost losses is insufficient in its own right to encourage some companies to restrict distributions to a level whereby operating capability is maintained in relation to the position at the beginning of the accounting period. Of course, the reduction of operating capability might be the policy of some companies.

Only ten companies in the survey adjusted current cost comparative figures, three disclosing adjusted comparatives and seven disclosing both adjusted and unadjusted figures. In all cases the retail price index was used. Furthermore, only seven companies produced five year summaries on a current cost basis, three showing the figures after adjustment by the retail price index and four without adjustment. One further company provided a five year summary of its historical cost results adjusted by the retail price index.

Other than the above, very little additional disclosure of current cost amounts was given, with only three companies providing information such as ratios or an analysis of the results in current cost terms. Even more significantly, only twelve companies commented on the results shown by the current cost accounts to a greater extent than by merely referring to the amounts reported therein. None of the 300 companies surveyed made any additional disclosure in respect of the change in shareholders' equity after allowing for the change in the general purchasing power of money, despite the fact that there is, internationally, a growing trend in inflation accounting favouring this form of statement.

The failure by several companies to disclose the reasons for non-compliance with SSAP 16, the few comments about the standard expressed in the accounts of those companies which complied and, as we have just discussed, the general absence of additional voluntary disclosures, inevitably means that the ASC will receive little guidance from company accounts when the Committee debates the way in which accounting for price-level changes should proceed.

EXAMPLE

A comprehensive set of supplementary current cost accounts prepared by Rothmans International p.l.c. is given below.

Example
Rothmans International p.l.c. *31 March 1982*
Consolidated Current Cost Accounts (£000):

Set out on the following pages are accounts prepared by reference to current cost principles in conformity with Statement of Standard Accounting Practice No. 16 and, as far as practicable, the related guidance notes. Under this method of accounting adjustments are made to the historic accounts to allow for the impact of price changes specific to the business when reporting assets employed and profits thereon.

Current cost accounting principles recognise that the operating assets have to be maintained at current values before profits can be determined. Assets are stated in the balance sheet at their value to the business. The current cost operating profit is the surplus, before interest and taxation, arising from the ordinary activities of the business in the period. It is determined after allowing for the impact of price changes on the productive assets employed in the business (the "net operating assets") but does not take into account the way in which these assets are financed.

Financing costs, after taking account of a gearing adjustment which reflects the extent to which price changes are financed externally by net borrowing, together with taxation and minority interests are deducted from the current cost operating profit to arrive at the current cost profit attributable to shareholders of the Company.

The adjustments made to the historic cost accounts are described in note 27 (*c*). Appropriate methods to arrive at the relevant adjustments continue to be developed. In particular, a single working capital adjustment is now calculated which combines the previously separate cost of sales and monetary working capital adjustments. This allows for the maintenance of working capital throughout the business cycle from the payment for raw materials to the receipt of sales debtors. As explained in the accompanying notes, there are differences in the methods adopted by Group companies, particularly in the determination of asset values and lives, and in some instances broad estimates have been used.

Below is a comparison of certain key information based on the historic cost accounts ("HCA") and current cost accounts ("CCA").

| | 1982 | | 1981 | |
	HCA	**CCA**	HCA	CCA
Operating profit	**131,871**	**61,342**	101,436	74,219
Profit before extraordinary item attributable to shareholders of Rothmans International p.l.c.	**47,323**	**16,815**	20,165	8,554
Earnings per share:				
Basic	**30·2p**	**10·7p**	12·9p	5·5p
Fully diluted	**18·3p**	**5·2p**	9·5p	4·8p
Dividend cover:				
Basic	**6·9**	**2·4**	3·5	1·5
Fully diluted	**4·2**	**1·2**	2·6	1·3
Tangible assets attributable to Ordinary shareholders of Rothmans International p.l.c.	**232,768**	**395,175**	161,836	288,829
Net tangible assets per share:				
Basic	**£1·49**	**£2·53**	£1·03	£1·85
Fully diluted	**£1·17**	**£1·69**	£0·94	£1·34

Consolidated current cost profit and loss account (£000):

	Notes	1982	1981
Sales revenue		**2,766,715**	2,384,618
Historic cost operating profit of the company and subsidiaries		**107,711**	85,140
Less: Current cost operating adjustments	27(c) & 28	**66,482**	23,758
		41,229	61,382
Share of current cost operating profits of associated companies	29	**20,113**	12,837
Current cost operating profit		**61,342**	74,219
Interest payable less receivable		**(13,913)**	(17,825)
Interest on convertible bonds		**(12,732)**	(12,360)
Gearing adjustment	27(d) & 28	**29,224**	8,586
		2,579	(21,599)
Current cost profit before taxation		**63,921**	52,620
Taxation	27(e)	**40,786**	35,248
		23,135	17,372
Minority interests		**6,320**	8,818
		16,815	8,554
Extraordinary item	30	**1,692**	—
Current cost profit attributable to shareholders of the company		**18,507**	8,554
Dividends		**6,898**	5,724
Retained current cost profit of the year	34	**11,609**	2,830
Earnings per share, before extra-ordinary item:	31		
Basic		**10·7p**	5·5p
Fully diluted		**5·2p**	4·8p

The notes set out on pages .. to .. form an integral part of these accounts.

Consolidated current cost balance sheet:

	Notes	1982		1981	
Net operating assets					
Fixed assets	27(f) & 32		**431,637**		376,955
Investments	27(h) & 33		**84,008**		60,557
Working capital					
Stocks	27(i)	**542,688**		454,382	
Debtors		**271,929**		229,351	
		814,617		683,733	
Less: Creditors and provisions		**386,232**		344,729	
			428,385		339,004
			944,030		776,516

Financed by

Shareholders' funds, including current cost reserve	27(j)		
Ordinary shareholders' tangible funds	34	**395,175**	288,829
Minority interests		**227,906**	178,706
		623,081	467,535
Preference share capital		**300**	300
Proposed dividend		**5,085**	4,146
Total shareholders' funds		**628,466**	471,981
Convertible bonds		**139,868**	133,412
Deferred taxation		**16,637**	12,232
Current taxation		**9,085**	14,658
Loans, net bank borrowings less short term securities	35	**67,625**	76,178
Provisions for employees' pensions		**82,349**	68,055
Net borrowing		**315,564**	304,535
		944,030	776,516

The notes set out on pages . . to . . form an integral part of these accounts.

Notes on current cost accounts:

27 Current Cost Accounting Policies

(a) Current Cost Accounts

The accounts on pages . . to . . are prepared on current cost principles and are supplementary to the historic cost accounts. The current cost convention is based on the principle of providing for the maintenance of the net operating assets of the Group's businesses, having regard to the extent to which those assets are financed externally by net borrowing.

The accounting policies used in the preparation of the historic cost accounts set out in note . . on pages . . and . . are followed in preparing the current cost accounts but are adapted, where appropriate, to conform with current cost principles.

(b) Foreign Currencies

The current cost accounts of overseas subsidiaries and associated companies are prepared in local currency and translated into sterling at the closing rate of exchange. Translation differences arising on the restatement of revaluation surpluses are reflected as a movement in current cost reserves.

(c) Current Cost Operating Adjustments

Two adjustments are made to remove holding gains, or losses, arising from changes in the current cost of assets consumed in production from the date of acquisition to their ultimate realisation in sales of the Group's products.

The depreciation adjustment represents the difference between the average current cost of the proportion of fixed assets consumed in the period and the depreciation charge in the historic cost accounts. Asset lives have not been adjusted. The restatement to current cost of the accumulated depreciation arising in prior years is charged to the current cost reserve.

The working capital adjustment measures holding gains or losses by reference to the price movements experienced by Group companies and the period that cost of sales is financed by the Group. This adjustment has the effect of allowing for the increase or decrease in the working capital employed in day-to-day operations as a result of changing prices.

(d) **Gearing Adjustment**
A proportion, called the gearing proportion, of the net operating assets of the business is financed externally by net borrowing. As the obligation to repay net borrowing is fixed in monetary amount, irrespective of price changes, it is unnecessary to provide for the impact of price changes on the proportion of net operating assets that is financed in this manner. Accordingly a gearing adjustment is applied which abates the current cost operating adjustments of each operating Group by their average gearing proportion at the balance sheet date.

(e) **Taxation**
Provisions for taxation, including deferred taxation, are the same in both the historic and current cost accounts.

(f) **Fixed Assets**
The gross current cost of fixed assets is recorded at current replacement cost or economic value if lower and is derived as follows:

Land and general purpose buildings are stated at open market valuation arrived at by the directors with, in appropriate instances, the help of independent professional advice.

Specialised buildings (mainly breweries) are stated at net current replacement cost.

Oil and gas properties are stated at the estimated future net income from proven and probable reserves together with an amount in respect of unproven land holdings.

Machinery, equipment and vehicles are stated at current replacement cost. For the most part, the gross cost of specialised production machinery and equipment is restated using indices constructed by Group companies appropriate to the plant concerned, taking into account technological change where necessary. Non production equipment, mainly office furniture and motor vehicles, is generally restated using government indices.

There are certain inconsistencies in the methods adopted by individual Group members to arrive at the gross current costs of fixed assets.

(g) **Intangible Assets**
No value is placed on intangible items, principally trade marks, and goodwill arising on consolidation which is deducted from shareholders' funds.

(h) **Associated Companies and Other Investments**
Investments in associated companies are stated at the attributable share of the net tangible assets as adjusted to a current cost basis. Other investments are stated at market value, where listed, or at directors' valuation.

(i) **Stocks**
Stocks and work in progress are included in the consolidated balance sheet at their value to the business, having regard to replacement costs and their net realisable values.

(j) **Current Cost Reserve**
The adjustments included in the current cost accounts are reflected in the current cost reserve, the balance of which represents the amounts set aside by the Group since 1st April 1978 to maintain the net operating assets of its businesses.

28 Summary of Current Cost Adjustments	1982	1981
Adjustments to operating profit		
For depreciation	18,419	14,451
For fixed asset disposals	1,880	715
	20,299	15,166
For working capital (including stocks)	46,183	8,592
The Company and its subsidiaries	66,482	23,758
Share of associated companies' current cost operating adjustments	4,047	3,459
	70,529	27,217
Gearing adjustment		
The Company and its subsidiaries	28,765	7,874
Share of associated companies' gearing adjustments	459	712
	29,224	8,586
Adjustments to profit before taxation	41,305	18,631
Minority interests	10,797	7,020
	30,508	11,611
Adjustment to extraordinary item (net of minority interests)	919	—
Attributable current cost adjustments	31,427	11,611

29 Share of Current Cost Operating Profits of Associated Companies		
	1982	1981
Share of historic cost operating profits	24,160	16,296
Less: Share of current cost operating adjustments	4,047	3,459
	20,113	12,837

30 Extraordinary Item			
As shown in the historic cost accounts		2,611	—
Current cost adjustment	1,532		
Less: Minority interests	613		
		919	—
		1,692	—

31 Current Cost Earnings per Share

The basic current cost earnings per share are calculated by reference to (a) current cost earnings, before the extraordinary item but after deducting preference dividends, of 16,801 (1981: 8,540) and (b) 18,259,456 Ordinary and 138,186,221 "B" Ordinary shares in issue for 1982 and 1981.

The fully diluted current cost earnings per share are based on adjusted earnings of 16,246 (1981: 15,049) and a revised total of 18,259,456 Ordinary and 297,163,999 "B" Ordinary shares. This allows for full conversion into 158,977,778 "B" Ordinary shares of the convertible bonds issued by Rothmans International p.l.c.

32 Fixed Assets

Machinery, equipment and vehicles

Gross current replacement cost	**633,695**	540,941
Less: Accumulated depreciation	**430,139**	357,296
Net current replacement cost	**203,556**	183,645
Land and buildings, including oil and gas properties	**228,081**	193,310
	431,637	376,955

33 Investments

Investments in associated companies

Shares and loans at cost	**18,971**	18,908
Less: Premium paid in excess of attributable net tangible assets at date of acquisition	**6,023**	6,023
	12,948	12,885
Share of post-acquisition retained profits and reserves		
Current cost reserve	**21,064**	15,691
Other	**43,073**	25,483
Attributable net tangible assets	**77,085**	54,059
Other investments	**6,923**	6,498
Total as shown in consolidated current cost balance sheet	**84,008**	60,557

45

34 Ordinary Shareholders' Funds and Minority interests

	Notes	1982 Current Cost Reserve	1982 Other Funds	1981 Current Cost Reserve	1981 Other Funds
Balance at 1st April					
Attributable to the Company		**151,384**	**137,445**	114,035	141,233
Attributable to minority shareholders		**75,938**	**102,768**	69,378	105,513
		227,322	**240,213**	183,413	246,746
Net exchange gains/(losses) on foreign currency assets and liabilities		**31,514**	**29,449**	(8,489)	(14,471)
Retained current cost profit of the year					
Attributable to the Company		**—**	**11,609**	—	2,830
Attributable to minority shareholders		**—**	**2,213**	—	4,914
Current cost revaluation surpluses arising during the year					
Realised and set aside to maintain net operating assets in arriving at					
Profit before taxation	28	**41,305**	**—**	18,631	—
Extraordinary item	30	**1,532**	**—**	—	—
Net movement on unrealised revaluations		**31,304**	**—**	34,466	—
Other movements in reserves		**(2,606)**	**9,226**	(699)	194
		330,371	**292,710**	227,322	240,213
Less: Attributable to minority shareholders		**109,350**	**118,556**	75,938	102,768
Balance at 31st March		**221,021**	**174,154**	151,384	137,445
		395,175		288,829	

Comprising:

	1982	1981
Ordinary shareholders' tangible funds as shown in the historic cost accounts	**232,768**	161,836
Unrealised revaluation surpluses		
Land and buildings, including oil and gas properties	**115,975**	92,039
Machinery, equipment and vehicles	**74,390**	63,423
Stocks	**42,246**	21,238
Investments	**10,420**	10,621
	243,031	187,321
Less: Attributable to minority shareholders	**80,624**	60,328
	162,407	126,993
Ordinary Shareholders' Tangible Funds at 31st March	**395,175**	288,829

Note: Amounts shown under "Other Funds" at 31st March 1982 and 31st March 1981 include Ordinary share capital 19,556, share premiums 30,415 and capital redemption reserve fund 1,000. The balance of "Other Funds" comprises the retained current cost earnings of the Company and subsidiaries and the Group's share of post-acquisition retained current cost profits and reserves of associated companies (note 33).

35 Loans, Net Bank Borrowings less Short Term Securities

		1982		1981
Medium and long term loans		**53,833**		45,470
Net bank borrowing				
Short term borrowings	**152,569**		144,028	
Less: Bank balances	**87,159**		55,086	
	———	**65,410**	———	88,942
		119,243		134,412
Less: Short term securities		**51,618**		58,234
		67,625		76,178

FURTHER READING

Accounting Standards Committee, SSAP 16, "Current Cost Accounting", London, March 1980.

Accounting Standards Committee, Guidance Notes on SSAP 16, "Current Cost Acounting", London, 1980.

Accounting Standards Committee, "CCA – The Easy Way", London, 1980.

Accounting Standards Committee, "Interim Report of the CCA Monitoring Working Party (The Neville Report)", London, 1983.

"Company Accounting and Disclosure – A Consultative Document", (Cmnd. 7654), HMSO, London, 1979.

"Companies Act 1981" Ch. 62, HMSO, London.

Frishkoff, P., "Financial Reporting and Changing Prices: A Review of Empirical Research", Research Report FASB, Stamford, Connecticut, 1982.

Inflation Accounting Committee (Sandilands), "Inflation Accounting" (Cmnd. 6225), HMSO, London, 1975.

Lee, T.A., "Income and Value Measurement", Second Edition, Nelson, London, 1980.

Mallinson, D., "Understanding Current Cost Accounting", Butterworths, London, 1980.

Tweedie, D. P., "Financial Reporting, Inflation and the Capital Maintenance Concept", International Centre for Research in Accounting, University of Lancaster, Occasional Paper No. 19, 1979.

Westwick, C.A., "The Lessons to be Learned from the Development of Inflation Accounting in the UK", *Accounting and Business Research*, Autumn 1980, pp. 353–373.

Whittington, G., "Inflation Accounting: An Introduction to the Debate", Cambridge University Press, 1983.

FIXED ASSETS

J. P. Carty

INTRODUCTION

This section deals with the valuation, presentation and depreciation of tangible fixed assets, including investment property, in historical cost accounts and current cost accounts.

It is important for a user of financial statements to understand how fixed assets have been accounted for because:—

(a) fixed assets constitute a material proportion of the net assets of many companies;

(b) there are a number of options open to companies in valuing and depreciating fixed assets. To evaluate the trend of a company's performance over time and to make valid comparisons between the performance of one company and another it is necessary to understand, and if need be adjust, the treatment accorded to fixed assets;

(c) many standard ratios used in the appraisal of performance, such as return on capital employed (ROCE), are materially affected by the way in which fixed assets are evaluated;

(d) gearing ratios, which are often taken into account when credit worthiness is assessed, may be substantially changed by a revaluation;

(e) when planning a takeover, the bidding company will expect to pay, as a rule of thumb, the minimum price of net asset per share values plus a premium to encourage shareholders to part with their shares;

(f) the shares of property investment companies are often evaluated on the basis of net assets per share; and

(g) the methods of depreciation adopted have an impact on the profit for the year.

REQUIREMENTS

Statutory requirements

The legal requirements concerning fixed assets have been made more detailed, but not significantly different, by the Companies Act 1981 which introduced a new Schedule 8 into the Companies Act 1948. The revised Schedule 8 applies to financial statements for periods commencing after 15 June 1982. They did not therefore apply to all companies in the survey, although in some instances they were adopted on a voluntary basis. The main requirements are:

(a) fixed assets must be categorised as Intangible Assets, Tangible assets or Investments;

(b) fixed assets must be stated at purchase price or production cost, or if the alternative valuation rules are applied at market value at the date of their last valuation or at current cost;

(c) fixed assets having a limited useful economic life must be depreciated systematically over their useful economic life; and

(d) the disclosure requirements include:—

(i) the cost or revalued amount at the beginning and end of the period;

(ii) movements on the cost or revalued amount during the year and on the depreciation balances;

(iii) the year and amount of revaluations of assets; and

(iv) for assets revalued in the period the names or qualifications of the valuers and the bases of valuation.

Standard accounting practice

SSAP 12 'Accounting for depreciation' was implemented in 1978 and applied to all financial statements covered by the survey. The standard requires that 'Provision for depreciation of fixed assets having a finite useful life should be made by allocating the cost or revalued amount less estimated residual values of the assets as fairly as possible to the periods expected to benefit from their use.' The standard requires disclosure for each major class of depreciable asset of the depreciation methods used and the useful lives or depreciation rates used. The explanatory notes in the standard state that buildings should be depreciated having regard to the same criteria as in the case of other fixed assets.

SSAP 19 'Accounting for investment properties' applies to all financial statements for periods starting on or after 1 July 1981. An investment property is an interest in land and/or buildings which is let to produce a rental income and is held for its investment potential. Properties occupied by a subsidiary company are excluded from the standard.

The standard requires that an investment property should not be depreciated but should be valued annually at open market value and the valuation incorporated into the financial statements.

SSAP 16 'Current cost accounting' requires that tangible fixed assets should be shown at their 'value to the business' and that depreciation should be calculated on the 'proportion of the value to the business consumed in the period.' The standard is not prescriptive about the methods to be adopted when preparing current cost accounts. In the case of land and buildings it is suggested that individual valuations should be the standard approach to establishing values and that plant and machinery should be valued by reference to indices.

The Assets Valuation Standards Committee of The Royal Institution of Chartered Surveyors has published a series of 'Guidance notes on the valuation of assets' which give advice on the valuation of assets for accounting purposes.

International standards

The International Accounting Standards Committee issued IAS 4 'Depreciation accounting' in 1976. In all material respects i is similar to SSAP 12, however, it does not deal with investment properties.

There are no standards in the USA or Canada specifically dealing with fixed assets and depreciation, although the topic is mentioned in a number of standards. However it is a generally accepted practice that fixed assets should be recorded at cost and assets with a limited useful life should be depreciated, including buildings.

The member states of the European Economic Community are in the process of implementing the 4th Directive on company accounts, which has already been brought into force in the UK through the Companies Act 1981.

The Australian standard on 'Depreciation of non-current assets', issued in 1974 requires the depreciation of buildings. The South African standard on 'Depreciation accounting' issued in 1982 does not require buildings to be depreciated but does include coverage of investment properties. An exposure draft has recently been issued in New Zealand on 'Investment properties' closely following the provisions of SSAP 19.

The Institute of Chartered Accountants of India issued AS 6 in 1982 on 'Depreciation accounting', which closely follows IAS 4. At present standards in India are regarded as recommendations and not as mandatory. The Sri Lankan government has recently issued a new Companies Act in which the disclosure requirements are drawn from the UK Companies Acts 1949 to 1980.

ANALYSIS

Presentation

Statutory and other information on fixed assets is normally disclosed in annual reports as follows:

Directors' Reports – particulars of significant changes in fixed assets during the year, details of revaluations made during the year, statements on the difference between the market value of interests in land and the amount at which they are included in the balance sheet which the directors consider should be drawn to the attention of shareholders.

Statement of Accounting Policies – the accounting policies for dealing with items which are judged material including the bases of valuation of fixed assets, depreciation policies and the treatment of government grants.

Notes to the Accounts – schedule of movements on fixed assets, analysis of property into freehold and leasehold properties, valuations included in the amounts for fixed assets, details of current valuations and values.

The main variation on the above pattern of disclosure is to concentrate the detailed information into the fixed assets schedule in the notes to the accounts.

Disclosure of the bases of valuation of fixed assets in current cost accounts is normally given in notes that supplement those accounts.

Classification of fixed assets

All companies in the survey appeared to meet the statutory requirements to analyse interests in property between freehold and leasehold property by having classifications within the fixed asset schedule in the notes, except in five instances where the information was provided by way of note.

Table 1 analyses the number of classifications that companies used for fixed assets other than those assets classified as freehold or leasehold property. The most common classification embraced plant, equipment and vehicles. Where two classifications were provided typically they were for plant and equipment with a separate classification of vehicles. Other classifications included mining assets 10, ships 6, aircraft 4, rental assets 8 and plant in the course of construction 3.

In CCA statements companies in the survey gave less detailed information about fixed assets merging them into wider classifications than for HC accounts.

Table 1 **Number of classifications used for fixing assets other than property**

| | 1982–83 | | | | | | | | 1981–82 | |
| | Large listed | | Medium listed | | Large unlisted | | Total | | Total | |
	HC	CCA	HC	CCA	HC	CCA	HC	CCA	HC	CCA
Number of companies.......	*100*	*100*	*150*	*150*	*50*	*50*	*300*	*300*	*300*	*300*
	%	%	%	%	%	%	%	%	%	%
Number of classifications:										
None (Note 2)...	—	3	—	10	—	8	—	7	—	8
One	64	66	68	67	50	20	64	59	68	69
Two	27	17	25	10	38	6	27	12	24	14
Three	8	3	6	3	12	—	8	3	6	2
Four or more....	1	1	1	—	—	—	1	—	2	—
CCA not prepared	—	10	—	10	—	66	—	19	—	7
	100	100	100	100	100	100	100	100	100	100

Notes:
1. Mineral assets, which may include properties, are included in the above table.
2. No analysis is given in the CCA statements between property and other fixed assets.
3. The differences shown in this table, between the results of the three groupings of company on the HC basis, are not statistically significant. They become significant on the CCA basis as only one-third of the unlisted companies published CCA statements.

Valuation of fixed assets in HCA

Companies revaluing all or part of their properties gave the names of the valuers or their qualifications. The valuation basis adopted was given as open market value in 17 instances, open market value for existing use in 9 instances and valuation with a view to disposal in 4 instances. In 2 cases the phrase 'assuming vacant possession' was added to the explanation of the bases of valuation.

8 companies said that it was their policy to revalue properties every three or five years. 3 companies indicated that they intended to carry out a valuation in the following year and 2 companies said that they had decided not to carry out a valuation owing to uncertainty in market conditions. 10 companies explained that as their properties were fully utilised in the business it was not appropriate, or was meaningless, to undertake a valuation.

Table 2　　　　**Revaluations of properties during the current accounting period**

| | 1982–83 | | | | 1981–82 |
Number of companies	Large listed 100	Medium listed 150	Large unlisted 50	Total 300	Total 300
	%	%	%	%	%
Revaluations:					
81 – 100%	6	10	16	9	8
61 – 80%	1	1	—	1	2
41 – 60%	2	1	2	2	1
21 – 40%	1	3	—	2	2
1 – 20%	18	11	4	12	11
	28	26	22	26	24
Data not available	2	2	2	2	5
	30	28	24	28	29
No revaluations	70	72	76	72	71
	100	100	100	100	100

Notes:
1. The percentage is calculated from the amount of the revaluation and the amount shown as 'cost or valuation' for the class of asset before depreciation, but after the revaluation is incorporated.
2. Whilst the surplus on revaluation was disclosed not all companies disclosed the proportion of assets revalued in the period.

Table 2 analyses the extent to which companies have carried out revaluations of properties during the current year. As in past years the results show that revaluations tend to be concentrated at the highest and lowest levels. Many of the partial revaluations are accounted for by the requirement of foreign governments whereby companies are required to revalue them as part of local statutory enactments.

Revaluations of plant and machinery are less frequent than revaluations of properties. 4 companies revalued all their plant during the year, 1 revalued 40% and 8 less than 20%.

The tabulated results do not include instances where companies had revalued the fixed assets of subsidiaries acquired during the year.

Table 3 analyses the proportion of properties that has been revalued at some date up to and including the current year, expressed as a percentage of the cost or valuation figure before depreciation.

Table 3   Property revaluations as a proportion of total values

	Large listed	Medium listed	Large unlisted	Total	Total
		1982–83			*1981–82*
Number of companies	*100*	*150*	*50*	*300*	*300*
	%	%	%	%	%
Total revaluations:					
81 – 100%	24	33	22	28	27
61 – 80%	19	16	10	16	17
41 – 60%	8	5	4	6	13
21 – 40%	11	9	2	9	6
1 – 20%	12	13	8	12	11
	74	76	46	71	74
Data not available	8	5	14	7	6
	82	81	60	78	80
Assets at cost	18	19	40	22	20
	100	100	100	100	100

Note: The results shown in this table, between the revaluations of properties for the three categories of company, are not statistically significant.

The results in Table 3 show that the large unlisted companies carried properties at a valuation less frequently than either the large or medium sized listed companies.

34 companies carried plant and machinery at valuations. In 16 instances the valuations accounted for less than 20% of total values. 25 of the companies were in the large listed companies and only 1 was in the large unlisted category.

Government grants

Under SSAP 4 'The accounting treatment of government grants', grants relating to fixed assets should be credited to revenue over the expected useful life of the asset either by reducing the cost of the acquisition by the grant or by treating the grant as a deferred credit a portion of which is taken to revenue annually.

Analysis of the policies adopted by companies in the survey showed that 76 companies (1981-82: 83) deduct grants direct from the cost of assets and 72 companies (1981–82: 80) carry the grant forward as a deferred credit. Two companies said that they transferred the grant to revenue over a stated number of years, presumably the life of the assets, whilst the remainder indicated that the grant was extinguished over the useful life. There was no difference between the methods adopted in the three categories of company surveyed.

Directors' statements on the market value of property

The Companies Act 1976 requires directors to state in their report if there have been any significant changes in fixed assets of the company during the year. If the market value of land is substantially different from the value carried in the balance sheet, and in the opinion of the directors the difference is of such significance that it should be reported to shareholders, then the difference should be indicated with as much precision as is practicable.

It is therefore left to the directors to decide what disclosures need to be made and the extent to which quantified differences need to be revealed.

The most common way of indicating changes in fixed assets during the year was to include a statement in the directors' report saying that changes in fixed assets were shown in a note to the accounts. Table 4 analyses the number and type of statements made by directors on the market value of property. The criterion adopted for compiling this table was whether or not a statement clarified the extent to which the book values of property differ from the market values. A statement on valuations made during the year which were incorporated into the accounts was not a relevant statement for this purpose. A statement about valuations which were not incorporated into the accounts is a relevant statement.

Table 4   Directors' statements on the market value of property

| | 1982–83 | | | | 1981–82 |
	Large listed	Medium listed	Large unlisted	Total	Total
Number of companies	100	150	50	300	300
	%	%	%	%	%
Statements made by directors on market values and book values to the effect that:					
a substantial difference exists – quantified	16	13	2	12	19
a substantial difference exists – not quantified	6	8	6	7	5
no substantial difference exists	10	14	—	10	12
market value is not less than book value	9	11	2	9	11
	41	46	10	38	47
As assets are fully utilised in the business of the company any difference between market value and book value is not significant	2	1	2	2	2
Other reasons for directors not giving a reason	1	4	4	3	1
	44	51	16	43	50
Companies not making a statement on the market value of property	56	49	84	57	50
	100	100	100	100	100

Note: The differences shown in this table, between the frequency of statements for the listed and unlisted categories of company, are statistically significant.

The results in Table 4 show that statements about the market values of properties are made less frequently by the unlisted than listed companies.

The results in Table 4 need to be considered together with the results in Table 3. If the two are read together it will be seen that a large proportion of companies in the survey either revalued their properties and incorporated the revaluation into the balance sheet or made a statement in the directors' report about the market value of properties.

Investment property

This is the first year in which SSAP 19 has applied to any companies in the survey. 166 companies were required to comply with the standard, whilst the remainder could have done so on a voluntary basis.

The standard now includes a definition of an investment property whereas in earlier years it was up to the companies to draw up their own definition. The designations of properties may therefore have changed over the year.

The provisions of the standard are not rigid, as part of the definition an investment property is 'held for its investment potential'. Companies may hold properties which they are renting out but which they may need to use for their own purposes at some future date. These properties may not be classified as investment properties.

The accounting treatment in SSAP 19 is a departure from the normal provisions of the Companies Acts which require buildings to be depreciated. The treatment of properties as investment properties under the terms of the standard is justified on the grounds that a departure from the normal provisions is necessary in order to give a true and fair view which is an overriding consideration. Where the treatment in SSAP 19 is followed the Companies Act 1948 (as revised) requires that particulars of the departure; the reasons for the departure and its effects shall be given in a note to the financial statements.

The disclosure concerning investment properties are analysed in Table 5.

Table 5   Investment properties – bases of balance sheet valuations

	1982–83				1981–82
	Large listed	Medium listed	Large unlisted	Total	Total
Number of companies	100	150	50	300	300
	%	%	%	%	%
Valuation at open market value in the current year	5	7	10	7	2
Valuation in earlier years	—	—	2	—	2
Partly at valuation and partly at cost.....................	1	—	—	—	—
Cost with open market valuation disclosed	—	—	—	—	1
Cost	—	1	4	2	1
Insufficient information	—	—	—	—	6
	6	8	16	9	12
No investment properties shown	94	92	84	91	88
	100	100	100	100	100

Note: The differences shown in this table, between the three categories of company, are not statistically significant.

Two of the companies which showed properties at cost acknowledged that their treatment was a departure from SSAP 19. Of all the companies which followed the treatment in the standard, and thus departed from the normal procedures of the Companies Act, only 3 gave explanations for the departure.

The standard requires that the carrying value of investment properties and the investment revaluation reserve should be displayed prominently in the financial statements. 4 companies showed investment properties as a separate line in the balance sheet or table of fixed assets movements in the notes, the remainder gave the information by way of a note. Only 3 companies showed a separate investment revaluation reserve. It appears that for most companies investment properties are not material in the context of their total operations.

Valuation of fixed assets in CCA

The bases of valuation to be used for fixed assets in current cost accounts are set out in SSAP 16 as statements of general principle. Companies are free to adopt a number of methods to arrive at 'value to the business'.

Inspection of the notes on the current cost accounts indicates that indices applied to the book values is the method almost universally adopted for plant and machinery. Valuation by the use of expert opinion for these assets is sometimes to be found, but is normally adopted for particular items of plant and machinery and not for asset classes as a whole.

The methods used to value property for CCA purposes are analysed in Table 6.

Table 6   **Methods used to determine CCA property values**

| | 1982–83 | | | | 1981–82 |
	Large listed	Medium listed	Large unlisted	Total	Total
Number of companies	100	150	50	300	300
	%	%	%	%	%
Current professional valuation	22	24	14	22	23
HCA values with a substantial revaluation in previous years adjusted by indices	23	18	—	17	8
HCA values with substantial re-valuations in previous years	8	13	4	10	11
HCA values adjusted by indices	14	6	8	9	16
HCA values with no recent substantial valuations	6	1	—	3	5
Directors' valuation	7	16	6	11	13
Mixture of valuation, indices or directors' estimation	6	4	—	4	9
Insurance values	1	—	—	—	1
	87	82	32	76	86
Insufficient data available	3	8	2	5	8
CCA not published	10	10	66	19	6
	100	100	100	100	100

Note: The differences shown in this table, between the three categories of company, are not statistically significant.

The professional valuations include valuations made by qualified employees of the company. In many instances valuations would be partly by external valuers and partly by internal valuers.

Depreciation

Depreciation is a material figure in the profit and loss account of most companies. The method of depreciation and the time period over which assets are depreciated are determined by the directors of a company. In view of the discretion allowed in this area the Companies Acts have required the total amount charged as depreciation in any period to be disclosed. SSAP 12 has increased the detail of disclosures by requiring information on particular classes of assets.

The straight line method of depreciation was adopted by 259 companies in the survey (1981–82: 252). 23 companies used a combination of methods (1981–82: 30) normally using the straight line method for most of their assets and the reducing balance method for one or more classes of asset. 3 companies used the sinking fund method for certain properties. 4 companies used a higher depreciation rate in the first year, then a constant rate thereafter. 1 company disclosed that it did not depreciate assets in the year of purchase whilst 1 company disclosed that it had provided for additional depreciation during the year, and disclosed the amount, because of uncertainty concerning the trading position. 18 companies (1981–82: 18) did not provide sufficient information to establish what depreciation methods had been used.

The disclosure methods of rates of depreciation or assumed lives presents difficulties. This disclosure is meant to give additional information to users of accounts but all too often the ranges of rates or years quoted is so large that the information is of little value. On the other hand companies appear to have problems summarising their multitude of practices for many different types of asset into a short note that will convey any meaning. Two companies revealed the average period over which buildings were depreciated and an average life over which plant and machinery was depreciated.

Table 7   Disclosure of depreciation rates or assumed lives of fixed assets

| | 1982–83 | | | | 1981–82 |
	Large listed	Medium listed	Large unlisted	Total	Total
Number of companies	*100*	*150*	*50*	*300*	*300*
	%	%	%	%	%
Depreciation rates or assumed lives disclosed for all or most assets	88	98	92	94	95
Depreciated over useful lives with no further details	7	1	4	3	—
No disclosure	5	1	4	3	5
	100	100	100	100	100

Note: The differences shown in this table, between the three categories of company, are not statistically significant.

58

Freehold buildings and long leasehold property still causes problems in the area of depreciation. The main reasons given for not depreciating buildings are either that the amount is not material or that the buildings are maintained in such a high state of repair that no depreciation has taken place. Five companies said that they depreciate buildings over the final fifty years of their anticipated life but it was not clear the extent to which some buildings were not being depreciated in the current period. One company disclosed that it was not practical to separate the cost of buildings from the cost of land so that it was calculating depreciation on the total cost of land and buildings.

Table 8   **Reasons given for not depreciating freehold building or long leasehold property**

| | 1982–83 | | | | 1981–82 |
	Large listed	Medium listed	Large unlisted	Total	Total
Number of companies	*100*	*150*	*50*	*300*	*300*
	%	%	%	%	%
The amount of depreciation is not material	1	2	4	2	8
Buildings are frequently re-valued	—	1	—	1	1
Market value exceeds the book value	—	—	—	—	1
Buildings are maintained to a high standard so that a depreciation charge is not necessary....................	5	4	4	4	—
	6	7	8	6	10
No reason given	—	2	4	2	2
Companies depreciating buildings......................	94	91	88	92	88
	100	100	100	100	100

Notes:
1. The above table includes companies which do not depreciate a specified part of their freehold or leasehold property.
2. The differences shown in this table, between the three categories of company, are not statistically significant.

One company disclosed that it had changed its policy and was depreciating buildings for the first time.

The rates of depreciation applied to buildings varied considerably. At the lower end of the scale one company depreciated buildings at the rate of ⅓rd of one per cent per annum, whilst at the top end of the scale 7 companies disclosed rates of 20 per cent. A significant proportion of companies disclosed a range of rates which they applied to buildings. The rates adopted are shown in Table 9.

Table 9 **Rates of depreciation applied to buildings**

	1982–83			
	Large listed	*Medium listed*	*Large unlisted*	*Total*
Number of companies	*100*	*150*	*50*	*300*
	%	%	%	%
1 per cent or less	8	6	6	7
Up to 2 per cent	39	58	56	51
Up to 3 per cent	12	13	6	12
Up to 4 per cent	4	2	6	12
More than 4 per cent	2	2	2	2
Multiple rates used	23	17	16	19
	88	98	92	94
Rates not disclosed	5	1	4	3
Depreciated over useful life	7	1	4	3
	100	100	100	100

Note: The differences shown in this table, between the rates of depreciation used by the three categories of company, are statistically significant.

The classification 'multiple rates' includes statements such as 'buildings are depreciated at rates of 1 per cent to 5 per cent per annum'.

The results disclosed in Table 9 show that large listed companies use multiple rates more commonly than other companies whilst the medium listed and large unlisted companies have a greater tendency to depreciate at rates close to 2 per cent per annum.

The rates of depreciation applied to plant and machinery again showed wide variations with multiple rates being disclosed by the majority of companies surveyed. The rates adopted are shown in Table 10.

Table 10 **Rates of depreciation applied to plant and machinery**

	1982–83			
	Large listed	*Medium listed*	*Large unlisted*	*Total*
Number of companies	*100*	*150*	*50*	*300*
	%	%	%	%
Up to 5 per cent	2	1	—	1
Up to 10 per cent	24	20	4	19
Up to 15 per cent	3	5	10	5
More than 15 per cent	2	6	22	8
Multiple rates used	57	66	56	61
	88	98	92	94
Rates not disclosed	5	1	4	3
Depreciated over useful life	7	1	4	3
	100	100	100	100

Notes:
1. The table shows the occasions when single rates are disclosed. The classification 'multiple rates' covers ranges as wide as 3% – 40%.
2. The differences shown in this table, between the three categories of company, are statistically significant.

The results in the table show that where single rates are quoted they tend to be at a higher rate for the unlisted companies than for the listed companies.

The most commonly disclosed rates of depreciation for vehicles were 20 per cent and 25 per cent with the larger listed companies preferring the lower rate and the medium listed and large unlisted companies the higher rate. The lowest rate quoted was 6 per cent and the highest 40 per cent on a reducing balance basis.

Ships were depreciated at rates of between 4 per cent and 6⅔ per cent. The usual rate for depreciating computers was 20 per cent with examples being seen of 25 per cent and 33⅓ per cent. One company disclosed a special write down of computer equipment.

Asset lives for current cost accounts

Table 11 shows the extent to which companies in the survey re-assessed the lives adopted for fixed assets in preparing current cost accounts. 2 companies explained that there was a range of lives for fixed assets. In HC accounts they depreciated assets over a conservative period of time whilst for CCA they chose a time period more in the centre of the possible range of values. It is clear that companies are concerned not only with depreciating individual assets but have some consideration for the total depreciation charge.

Table 11   **Asset lives for current cost accounts**

	1982–83				1981–82
	Large listed	Medium listed	Large unlisted	Total	Total
Number of companies	100	150	50	300	300
	%	%	%	%	%
Same asset lives used in HC as in CCA	59	55	16	50	71
Different lives used for HC and CCA	16	16	4	14	17
	75	71	20	64	88
Information not disclosed	14	18	12	16	6
Only CCA published	1	1	2	1	—
No CCA published	10	10	66	19	6
	100	100	100	100	100

7 companies which adopt different lives for CCA provide depreciation on assets which are fully written off for HC purposes. 3 companies adopt reducing balance methods for depreciating in CCA accounts although they use straight line methods in HC. 1 company uses basically the same lives for both sets of accounts but in CCA charges a higher rate of depreciation in the first year with lower rates in subsequent years.

Example 1
George Wimpey PLC　　*31 December 1982*
Extract from the directors' report

Fixed Assets

No significant changes have occurred in the fixed assets, other than the inclusion of assets of subsidiaries acquired during the year and additions and disposals in the course of business. Properties owned by the group and used in its construction – related activities continue to be valued at cost. The board is of the opinion that the aggregate value of these properties is in excess of book value but this difference is not significant in relation to the affairs of the group as a whole.

Property Assets

The consolidated balance sheet incorporates the open market value of investment properties and investments in property companies and associated property companies.
　Investment properties have been professionally valued and are included on that basis.
　Investments in listed property companies are included at the quoted market share.
　In previous years the group's share of capital surpluses and reserves of its unlisted investment in The Oldham Estate Company PLC, and the group's share of capital surpluses of associated property companies, mainly Euston Centre Properties PLC, have not been shown in the notes on the accounts. These amounts in respect of 1982 would have been £54·3 million for Oldham and £66·7 million for Euston and other associated property companies.
　Under accounting standards, companies are required to consolidate their share of reserves of associated companies including surpluses on revaluation of fixed assets. However the directors have noted that in practice the market value of listed property companies falls short of the accumulated share capital and reserves of those companies. This shortfall has recently been about 40% and, in computing the 'market value' and on the grounds of prudence, this discount has been applied to the group's share of Oldham and Euston and other associated companies. Accordingly the amount taken into revaluation of Oldham is £32·6 million and of Euston and other associated property companies is £40·0 million.
　The investment property revaluation included in the 1982 balance sheet of the group is set out below.
　If the group took full account of its share of shareholders funds in Oldham and its share of the capital surpluses in associates, the amount of the total revaluation surpluses would be £143·1 million but the prudent discount of these investments reduces the total to £94·7 million.
　Because these assets are held as long term investments, it is the opinion of the directors that calculation of the contingent liability to taxation on such surpluses in the event of any disposals would not be appropriate.

Statement of Investment Property Revaluation

	Investments at cost £m	Revaluation surplus £m	Balance sheet value £m
Investment properties	68·0	19·2	87·2
Listed property investments	2·0	2·9	4·9
Unlisted property investment (Oldham) group share of shareholders funds £54·3 million less discount of 40% (cost £23,000)	—	32·6	32·6
Associated property companies (mainly Euston) including revaluation surpluses of £66·7 million less discount of 40%	3·9	40·0	43·9
Investment properties under construction not revalued	31·8	—	31·8
Dealing properties completed and under construction (not revalued in the accounts as they are classified as current assets)	30·5	—	30·5
	136·2	94·7	230·9

Extract from the Statement of Accounting Policies

4 Depreciation
Depreciation is provided on the original cost of assets in equal annual instalments, except in the case of quarries, on the bases set out below:

Offices and depots occupied by the group
  Freehold buildings and long leaseholds
    in excess of 50 years   Over 40 years
    Short leaseholds   Over the period of the lease
Quarries   By reference to the materials extracted
Plant and vessels   Over the expected useful life of the assets ranging mainly from 3 to 12 years

No depreciation is provided on investment properties in the United Kingdom.

Extract from the notes to the accounts

11 Tangible fixed assets continued
Land and buildings held as property investment (except for certain short leasehold properties) were professionally revalued during the year resulting in a surplus of £19·2 million (1981 nil) which has been credited direct to reserves. The valuation of UK and certain overseas properties was jointly undertaken by Gooch & Wagstaff, Chartered Surveyors and Collier & Madge, Chartered Surveyors, on the basis of open market value assuming existing use in accordance with the principles contained in the Guidance Notes on the Valuations of Property Assets issued by the Royal Institution of Chartered Surveyors. The valuations of other overseas properties have been carried out by local professional firms on the same basis.

Extract from the notes to the Current Cost Accounts

1 Accounting policies (where different from the historic accounts)

GENERAL BASIS OF ACCOUNTING
The supplementary current cost accounts have been prepared in accordance with the principles set out in the Statement of Standard Accounting Practice No. 16.

VALUATION OF ASSETS
(a) Trading properties: current market value on an existing use basis and by reference to internal and external valuations.
(b) Plant and equipment: by applying appropriate government indices, except some plant of a specialised nature by reference to replacement or internal valuation.
(c) The depreciation adjustment arises from applying the group's normal depreciation policies to the restated value of the tangible fixed assets except that trading properties are depreciated over the re-assessed expected useful lives not exceeding 40 years.
(d) Property investment and dealing entities remain at their value in the historic accounts because they are exempted by the standard.

FURTHER READING

Baxter, W.T., *Depreciation*, Sweet & Maxwell, 1971

FOREIGN CURRENCIES

S. J. Gray and C. B. Roberts

INTRODUCTION

Companies may be involved in two different types of foreign currency accounting. Firstly, an individual company may enter directly into transactions which are denominated in foreign currencies. This will involve the company in reporting the results of these transactions in the domestic currency in preparing its financial statements. Secondly, a group may have foreign operations, i.e. foreign subsidiaries, associated companies or branches. In order to consolidate the accounts of group companies denominated in different currencies it will be necessary, therefore, to translate the financial statements of such foreign enterprises into a common currency for reporting purposes.

Most of the debate in the area of foreign currency accounting has been concerned with the problem of translation of foreign currency financial statements in consolidated accounts. The debate relates to two major aspects: which exchange rate to use; and how to treat exchange gains and losses. There is a choice of possible exchange rates which can be used: in the main these are either the historical rate i.e. that ruling at the date the transaction occurred; or the closing rate i.e. the rate ruling at the balance sheet date. The use of these rates can lead to several possible methods, though the major methods now practiced are the 'closing rate/net investment' method and the 'temporal' method. The debate on which method to employ is based upon arguments concerning the purposes of both translation and consolidation.

The closing rate/net investment method is based upon the premise that the objective of consolidation is to present information useful to decision-makers in the parent country; but without necessarily presenting the results as if the parent and its subsidiaries are a single entity. If foreign subsidiaries are relatively independent then what is at risk from the parent's perspective is the net worth of the investment. Accordingly, it is important to retain the relationships existing in the subsidiaries accounts in reporting the change in the net worth due to exchange rate changes. This is done if all items are translated at the closing rate of exchange. Opponents of this method maintain that the translation of items at historical cost by a current rate of exchange results in meaningless numbers and that the method has been accepted by accountancy bodies in the UK and USA for the pragmatic reason that it is currently a very popular method. This popularity may be due in part to the fact that it is relatively simple to implement.

The temporal method, originally expounded in the USA in ARS 12 "Reporting foreign operations of US companies in US dollars" (1972) and later introduced in FASB 8 in 1975, now replaced by FASB 52 "Foreign currency translation", is based upon the premise that the objective of consolidation is to present the results of the parent company and its dependent subsidiaries as if it was a single entity. Parent company measurement bases are used throughout and the translation rate is determined by the measurement basis used. Accordingly, items valued at historical cost are translated at the historical rate and items valued at a current or future rate are translated at the closing rate.

There are a further two methods occasionally used in the UK and a number of other countries. These are the 'monetary/non-monetary' method, which translates monetary items at the closing rate and non-monetary items at the historical rate; and the 'current/non-current' method, which translates current assets and liabilities at the closing rate and non-current assets and liabilities at the historical rate.

The debate on the treatment of exchange gains/losses or differences hinges on whether they should be taken to the profit and loss account below or above the line, or to reserves. The argument for taking items to the profit and loss account is that profit should reflect all changes in the values of assets. However, taking gains or losses to the profit and loss account can result in very large fluctuations in results. This was very unpopular with companies especially under FASB 8 in the USA. Therefore, it was argued that they should be treated as extraordinary gains or losses. The problem here is that this is inconsistent with the definition of extraordinary item as items "expected not to recur frequently or regularly". Thus it is now generally agreed that under the temporal method, where subsidiaries are closely linked with the parent, exchange differences should be taken to trading profit. An alternative is to take such differences to reserves. This course of action has now been agreed upon for the closing rate method which has been adopted in both SSAP 20 "Foreign currency translation" in the UK and FASB 52 in the USA using the argument that the profit and loss account should reflect strictly the success of foreign operations as measured in the foreign subsidiaries' accounts.

REQUIREMENTS

Statutory requirements

The UK Companies Acts generally do not contain any detailed provisions regarding the accounting methods to be employed or detailed disclosure requirements in the area of foreign currency transactions and translation. Schedule 8A, paragraph 11 (9) and schedule 8, paragraph 58 (1) of the Companies Act 1948, as amended, require disclosure only of the bases used for the conversion of foreign currencies and the translation of sums originally denominated in foreign currencies respectively. There are no requirements covering such areas as the disclosure of the amounts involved and the treatment of exchange gains and losses arising from transactions and translation. However, information is required on any movement in reserves.

The Companies Act 1981, which was largely based upon the EEC 4th Directive, does not alter the existing requirements of the Companies Act and even the wording remains essentially unchanged. Nor does it increase the amount of information required to be disclosed in this area.

The next major UK Companies Act seems likely to be based upon the EEC 7th Directive on consolidated financial statements which was approved in June 1983. However, this Directive does not appear likely to alter the existing position in UK law as the Directive (Article 34 (1) requires only that:

> "For items included in the consolidated accounts which are or were originally expressed in foreign currency the bases of conversion used to express them in the currency in which the consolidated accounts are drawn up must be disclosed".

Thus both existing and foreseeable legislation requires only a policy statement, usually provided in the notes to the accounts, stating the method used for the conversion and/or translation of foreign currency items together with disclosure of the movement on reserves.

Standard accounting practice

There was no accounting standard on foreign currency translation effective during the period covered by the survey. However SSAP 20 "Foreign currency translation" was issued in April 1983 and is effective for accounting periods beginning on or after 1st April 1983. This will affect the type and quantity of information produced in future years. Before April 1983, the only accounting standard covering this area was SSAP 2 "Disclosure of accounting policies" which requires disclosure of the accounting policy for any material items, which in many cases will include foreign currency translation. At the same time, the existence of exposure drafts, ED 21 and ED 27, both on foreign currencies, the latter being substantially the same as the final accounting standard, may have influenced practice to some degree in advance of the accounting standard being introduced.

SSAP 20 is similar to the USA standard FASB 52 issued in December 1981. There are only very minor differences between them. Looking first at translation, SSAP 20 allows two methods, the 'closing rate/net investment' method and the 'temporal' method. However, the circumstances under which each is to be used are clearly laid down. Where foreign subsidiaries are separate entities with relatively little dependence upon the parent company, the objective of translation is to retain the relationships existing in the subsidiaries' accounts. Accordingly, balance sheet items are translated at the closing rate. Profit and loss account items are translated at either the average or closing rate, unlike FASB 52 which requires the use of the average rate only. All translation differences are taken directly to reserves. It is suggested in SSAP 20 that if such differences were taken to the profit and loss account then the profit figure would reflect both the success of foreign operations, as measured in the foreign currency, and the effects of exchange rate changes on the net investment, with misleading results.

A major feature of SSAP 20 is the use of the 'cover' concept whereby translation differences on foreign currency borrowings which have been used to finance, or provide a hedge against, individual company or group equity investments may be offset, subject to certain limitations, as reserve movements against translation differences arising from such investments.

The temporal method is used where the foreign subsidiary is closely integrated with and dependent upon the parent company. In the USA, the temporal method is also required to be used for subsidiaries in countries with "hyper-inflation". Under this method, all items are translated at the exchange rate ruling at the date of the relevant transaction or revaluation as recorded in the accounts and all exchange differences are taken directly to the profit and loss account.

As regards foreign currency "transactions" by individual companies, SSAP 20 requires these to be converted at the rate ruling at the date the transaction occurred. Any exchange gain or loss which then occurs due to a change in the exchange rate between the transaction being agreed upon and finally being settled or between the agreement date and the balance sheet date should be taken to the profit and loss account except under special circumstances.

Turning to the question of disclosure, in contrast to FASB 52 in the USA, companies are not required under SSAP 20 to disclose the net exchange gain or loss overall which is credited/charged to the profit and loss account. However, they must disclose the net movement on reserves arising from exchange differences. Furthermore, the net amount of exchange gains and losses offset to reserves and the net amount charged/credited to the profit and loss account in respect of foreign currency borrowings must also be disclosed.

International accounting standards

IAS 3 "Consolidated financial statements", issued in 1976, requires the disclosure of exposure to any exceptional risks of operating in foreign countries which explicitly includes the risk of foreign currency fluctuations. However, this subject was dealt with more fully in July 1983 when IAS 21 "Accounting for the effects of changes in foreign exchange rates" was issued. This will be effective only from January 1985. If companies comply with SSAP 20 then they will also comply with IAS 21. Both are very similar though the international standard is a little more flexible in its treatment of exchange gains and losses.

ANALYSIS

Accounting policies

The extent to which companies disclose their accounting policies in respect of the method of translation and the treatment of exchange differences in consolidated financial statements is given in Table 1. A total of 78% of companies disclosed both policies and this percentage increases to 90% if the sample is reduced by the 13% of companies with no evidence of foreign operations. Only 9 companies involved in foreign operations did not disclose the translation method used. However, in respect of the treatment of exchange differences the number not disclosing their policy increased to 27 companies. There is a higher level of non-disclosure for medium listed and large unlisted companies compared to large listed companies.

Table 1   Accounting policies for consolidated financial statements

		1982–83		
	Large listed	Medium listed	Large unlisted	Total
Number of companies	100	150	50	300
	%	%	%	%
Disclosed both translation method and treatment of exchange differences	94	75	56	78
Disclosed translation method only	2	8	8	6
Disclosed treatment of exchange differences only	–	–	–	–
Policy not disclosed	2	5	–	3
No evidence of foreign operations (Note 1)	2	12	36	13
	100	100	100	100

Notes:
1. Including one medium listed company with no consolidated foreign subsidiaries.
2. The differences shown in this table, between the levels of disclosure for the three categories of company, are statistically significant.

As regards accounting policies for transactions by individual companies, Table 2 shows that disclosure of the method used is very low relative to disclosure of the treatment of exchange differences. However, there is no difference in practice between the company groupings.

Table 2 Accounting policies for transactions of individual companies

	Large listed	Medium listed	Large unlisted	Total
	1982–83			
Number of companies	*100*	*150*	*50*	*300*
	%	%	%	%
Disclosed method used and treatment of exchange differences	6	5	8	6
Disclosed treatment of exchange differences only	55	46	30	46
Not disclosed........................	37	37	30	36
No evidence of foreign transactions (Note 1)	2	12	32	12
	100	100	100	100

Notes:
1. Including one medium listed company with no consolidated foreign subsidiaries.
2. The differences shown in this table, between the levels of disclosures for the three categories of company, are not statistically significant.

Translation methods

It can be seen from Table 3 that the closing rate method for balance sheet items is by far the most popular method having been adopted by 94% of companies with foreign operations. Only 7 companies used other methods including 2 employing the temporal method.

Table 3   Translation method used for balance sheet items

	Large listed	Medium listed	Large unlisted	Total
	1982–83			
Number of companies	*100*	*150*	*50*	*300*
	%	%	%	%
Closing rate method	92	81	62	81
Temporal method....................	1	–	2	1
Monetary/non-monetary method	1	1	–	1
Current/non-current method..........	1	1	–	1
Other method	1	–	–	–
Not disclosed......................	2	5	–	3
No evidence of foreign operations (Note 1)	2	12	36	13
	100	100	100	100

For Notes to table see overleaf.

Notes:
1. Including one medium listed company with no consolidated foreign subsidiaries.
2. The differences shown in this table, between the methods used by the three categories of company, are not statistically significant.

As regards profit and loss items (see Table 4), the closing rate is similarly popular but a large minority of 71 companies with foreign operations used the average rate instead for translation purposes. It is interesting to note that the newly introduced SSAP 20 is permissive on this point, reflecting no doubt the range of practice evident.

Table 4   **Translation method used for profit and loss items**

	1982–83			
	Large listed	Medium listed	Large unlisted	Total
Number of companies	*100*	*150*	*50*	*300*
	%	%	%	%
Closing rate	62	46	26	48
Average rate	25	24	20	24
Other method	5	3	–	3
Not disclosed	6	14	18	12
No evidence of foreign operations (Note 1)	2	13	36	13
	100	100	100	100

Notes:
1. Including one medium listed company with no consolidated foreign subsidiaries and one with foreign debt only.
2. The differences shown in this table, between the methods used by the three categories of company, are not statistically significant.

Treatment of exchange differences

1. Method of treatment

For those companies using the closing rate method for translating balance sheet items, an analysis of the treatment of exchange differences on consolidation is presented in Table 5. Consistent with what will be required under SSAP 20, the large majority of companies (68%) disclosing their treatment took such differences only to reserves. A further 10% took a proportion of exchange differences to reserves while a minority of 13% took them only to the profit and loss account. The large unlisted companies, however, exhibited a lower propensity (42%) to take exchange differences only to reserves.

Table 5   **Treatment of exchange differences on consolidation by companies using the closing rate method for balance sheet items**

| | *1982–83* | | | |
	Large listed	*Medium listed*	*Large unlisted*	*Total*
Number of companies	92	122	31	245
	%	%	%	.%
Taken only to the Profit and Loss Account	10	11	26	13
Taken only to Reserves	75	69	42	68
Taken both to the Profit and Loss Account and to Reserves	13	8	13	10
Not disclosed	2	12	19	9
	100	100	100	100

Note: The differences shown in this table, between the treatments used by the three categories of company, are statistically significant.

The pattern of treatment in respect of the closing rate method is maintained when the analysis is extended to all methods of translation (see Table 6). Though there is a lower overall percentage of companies taking exchange differences only to reserves there is no change in the finding concerning the practice of large unlisted companies.

Table 6   **Treatment of exchange differences on consolidation by all companies for all methods of translation**

| | *1982–83* | | | |
	Large listed	*Medium listed*	*Large unlisted*	*Total*
Number of companies	100	150	50	300
	%	%	%	%
Taken only to the Profit and Loss Account	11	12	22	13
Taken only to Reserves	71	56	26	56
Taken both to the Profit and Loss Account and to Reserves	12	7	8	9
Not disclosed	4	13	8	9
No evidence of foreign operations (Note 1)	2	12	36	13
	100	100	100	100

Notes:
1. Including one medium listed company with no consolidated foreign subsidiaries.
2. The differences shown in this table, between the treatments used by the three categories of company, are statistically significant.

As regards exchange differences on transactions, the practice is overwhelmingly to include these in the profit and loss account as can be seen in Table 7. At the same time, 41% of companies failed to disclose their method of treatment.

Table 7   Treatment of exchange differences on transactions of individual companies

| | *1982–83* | | | |
	Large listed	*Medium listed*	*Large unlisted*	*Total*
Number of companies	*100*	*150*	*50*	*300*
	%	%	%	%
Taken only to the Profit and Loss Account (Note 1)	53	47	30	47
Taken only to reserves	1	–	–	–
Taken both to the Profit and Loss Account and to Reserves	1	–	–	–
Not disclosed	43	41	38	41
No evidence of foreign transactions	2	12	32	12
	100	100	100	100

Notes:
1. Including two medium listed companies which state no policy but disclose the amount involved.
2. The differences shown in this table, between the treatments used by the three categories of company, are not statistically significant.

2. Disclosure of differences

By way of comparison with the disclosed accounting policies in respect of the treatment of exchange differences, it can be seen from Table 8 that the large majority of companies, consistent with what will be required under SSAP 20, revealed the net movement on reserves on account of exchange differences. At the same time, it should be noted that this information was not disclosed by a total of 24 companies.

Table 8 Disclosure of amount of exchange differences on translation in movement on reserves

	Large listed	Medium listed	Large unlisted	Total
	1982–83			
Number of companies	100	150	50	300
	%	%	%	%
Disclosed net movement on historical cost reserves	82	64	38	65
Not disclosed	5	11	4	8
Not applicable	13	25	58	27
	100	100	100	100

Note: The differences shown in this table, between the disclosures of the three categories of company, are not statistically significant.

Table 9 shows, however, that only half of the companies concerned disclosed the net gain or loss overall which is credited/charged to the profit and loss account. Such disclosure will not, however, be required under SSAP 20 despite the likely usefulness of this item of information to investors and others concerned about the impact of exchange differences on profits. It is interesting to note that this information is required under FASB 52 in the USA.

Table 9 Disclosure of amount of exchange differences on translation included in profit and loss account

	Large listed	Medium listed	Large unlisted	Total
	1982–83			
Number of companies	100	150	50	300
	%	%	%	%
Disclosed net gain or loss credited/charged to Profit and Loss Account (Note 1)	16	15	16	15
Not disclosed	11	16	22	15
Not applicable	73	69	62	70
	100	100	100	100

Notes:
1. Including three medium-sized and two private companies with no disclosed policy.
2. The differences shown in this table, between the disclosures of the three categories of company, are statistically significant.

On the other hand, disclosure of the amount of exchange differences on foreign currency borrowing is information which will be required under SSAP 20 and it is interesting to note from Table 10 that a small number of companies already disclose the amount offset in reserves and the amount charged/credited to the profit and loss account i.e. 19 companies and 11 companies respectively. These companies herald a substantial change in disclosure practices in the future.

Table 10 Disclosure of amount of exchange differences on translation of foreign currency borrowing

| | 1982–83 | | | |
	Large listed	Medium listed	Large unlisted	Total
Number of companies	*100*	*150*	*50*	*300*
	%	%	%	%
Disclosed gain or loss on foreign currency borrowing – amount offset in reserves	16	2	–	6
Disclosed gain or loss on foreign currency borrowing – amount charged to the Profit and Loss Account	5	3	2	4
Not disclosed.......................	44	22	8	27
Not applicable/No information	35	73	90	63
	100	100	100	100

Note: The differences shown in this table, between the disclosures of the three categories of company, are not statistically significant.

In contrast to the disclosed policy treatment of exchange differences on transactions by the majority of companies (see Table 2) it can be seen from Table 11 that only a small number of companies disclose the actual amounts of exchange differences concerned. Whether this information is considered sensitive or the amounts are not material is not clear.

Table 11   Disclosure of amount of exchange differences on transactions of individual companies

| | 1982–83 | | | |
	Large listed	Medium listed	Large unlisted	Total
Number of companies	*100*	*150*	*50*	*300*
	%	%	%	%
Disclosed exchange gain/loss...........	10	6	6	7
Not disclosed.......................	88	82	62	81
No evidence of foreign transactions	2	12	32	12
	100	100	100	100

Note: The differences shown in this table, between the disclosures of the three categories of company, are not statistically significant.

A further question regarding the treatment of exchange differences concerns the location of gains or losses taken to the profit and loss account. Of particular interest is whether such differences are taken above or below the line i.e. before extraordinary items or in/after extraordinary items, and whether there is any systematic treatment of gains or losses to smooth or enhance reported profits. Tables 12 and 13 analyse disclosed exchange differences on translation and transactions respectively from which no clear pattern emerges though the majority of companies include gains before or in extraordinary items. It should be noted, however, that the practice of including translation differences in the profit and loss account will be restricted in future following the introduction of SSAP 20.

Table 12   Disclosure of exchange differences on translation taken to the profit and loss account

	1982–83			
	Large listed	Medium listed	Large unlisted	Total
Number of companies	23	28	15	66
	%	%	%	%
Disclosed before extraordinary items: ...	39	14	33	27
companies reporting a gain	17	7	27	15
companies reporting a loss	22	7	6	12
Disclosed in extraordinary items:	26	64	14	40
companies reporting a gain	17	39	7	24
companies reporting a loss	9	25	7	15
Disclosed after extraordinary items:	4	—	7	3
companies reporting a gain	4		7	3
companies reporting a loss				
Taken to the profit and loss account but amount not disclosed	3	22	46	30
	100	100	100	100

Note: The differences shown in this table, between the disclosures of the three categories of company, are not statistically significant.

Table 13 Disclosure of exchange differences on transactions taken to the profit and loss account

	1982–83			
	Large listed	*Medium listed*	*Large unlisted*	*Total*
Number of companies	54	71	15	140
	%	%	%	%
Disclosed before extraordinary items: ...	9	8	20	10
companies reporting a gain	4	5	20	6
companies reporting a loss...........	5	3	–	4
Disclosed in extraordinary items:	9	2	–	5
companies reporting a gain	–	2		1
companies reporting an immaterial amount........................	2	–		1
companies reporting a loss...........	7	–		3
Taken to the Profit and Loss Account but amount not disclosed	82	90	80	85
	100	100	100	100

Note: The differences shown in this table, between the disclosures of the three categories of company, are not statistically significant.

Impact of exchange differences

In addition to questions of treatment of exchange differences there is the issue of the impact of such differences on profits and shareholders' equity. This is crucial in establishing the importance of accounting policy in this area for companies and external users. Table 14 shows that the average net movement in reserves is a gain of 14·22% of attributable profit and 1·45% of shareholders equity respectively for all companies. However, the range of impacts is quite considerable with large listed companies experiencing an average movement of 18·45% and a maximum of 746% of attributable profit compared to 10·46% and 508% with respect to medium listed companies and 14·77% and 183% for large unlisted companies.

Perhaps more important is the impact of exchange differences recorded in the profit and loss account. Table 15 shows that the average translation difference is a gain of 8·28% of attributable profit which is consistent with the findings regarding location reported in Tables 12 and 13. On the other hand, the average net transaction gain/loss is a loss of 0·37% of attributable profit. Again, the range of impacts varies but especially interesting is the relatively high impact in respect of large unlisted companies which show average gains of 10·13% and 11·22% for translation and transactions respectively.

Table 14 The impact of exchange differences: movement on reserves

1. Net movement on historical cost reserves

	1982–83			
	Large listed	Medium listed	Large unlisted	Total
Number of companies	82	95	19	196
	%	%	%	%
Mean as a percentage of attributable profit	18·45	10·46	14·77	14·22
Minimum....................	−1080·50	−484·99	−78·64	−1080·50
Maximum	746·02	508·10	183·40	746·02

2. Net movement on historical cost reserves

	1982–83			
	Large listed	Medium listed	Large unlisted	Total
Number of companies	82	95	19	196
	%	%	%	%
Mean as a percentage of opening shareholders equity	1·00	1·63	2·62	1·45
Minimum....................	−25·00	−5·53	−0·41	−25·00
Maximum	12·25	16·33	22·18	22·18

Table 15 The impact of exchange differences: profit and loss account
1. Net translation difference

	1982–83			
	Large listed	Medium listed	Large unlisted	Total
Number of companies	16	22	8	46
	%	%	%	%
Mean as a percentage of attributable profit	7·56	8·14	10·13	8·28
Minimum....................	−8·35	−71·58	−19·82	−71·58
Maximum	40·83	184·00	36·29	184·00

77

2. Net transaction gain or loss

	Large listed	Medium listed	Large unlisted	Total
	1982–83			
Number of companies	10	7	3	20
	%	%	%	%
Mean as a percentage of attributable profit	−7·43	3·62	11·22	−0·37
Minimum....................	−38·71	−7·59	1·14	−38·71
Maximum	7·05	24·33	21·11	24·33

Taken overall, this analysis tends to confirm that the impact of exchange differences is material and that in some cases they overshadow the results of operations. Further, where translation differences have been included in the profit and loss account, the overall effect has been to increase or under-pin profits rather than the reverse.

Disclosure of additional information

Additional information relevant to an assessment of exchange risks includes the disclosure of foreign debt, both long-term and short-term, foreign assets, and qualitative comment by Directors on the effects of exchange rate changes and on specific country risks.

1. Foreign debt

It can be seen from Table 16 that the majority of companies which disclose foreign debt disclose their long-term foreign loans analysed by currency; this is perhaps most appropriate from a risk analysis perspective. In contrast, 13% or 38 companies disclosed separate totals only of UK and foreign debt. In the case of 51% of companies there was insufficient information to assess whether or not their balance sheets included foreign debt. This poses a major problem of risk analysis at the present time.

Table 16 **Disclosure of foreign long-term debt**

	Large listed	Medium listed	Large unlisted	Total
	1982–83			
Number of companies	100	150	50	300
	%	%	%	%
Disclosed totals of U.K. and foreign debt	19	12	2	13
Disclosed loans by currency	43	14	8	23
Disclosed loans by country or continent	3	1	–	2
No foreign debt......................	–	8	44	11
Not applicable/No information	35	65	46	51
	100	100	100	100

Note: The differences shown in this table, between the disclosures of the three categories of company, are statistically significant.

As regards the importance of long-term foreign debt shown in Table 17, it is noteworthy that this is on average 51·30% of all long-term debt, with the highest average relating to large unlisted companies at 62·14%, and that in some instances this percentage becomes 100%.

Table 17   **Foreign long-term debt**

	1982–83			
	Large listed	Medium listed	Large unlisted	Total
Number of companies	65	41	5	111
	%	%	%	%
Mean as a percentage of total long-term debt	52·85	47·53	62·14	51·30
Minimum	1·15	3·32	25·33	1·15
Maximum	100·00	100·00	93·32	100·00

In contrast, the incidence of short-term foreign loans seems to be much lower as shown in Table 18. This may be an area where disclosure tends to be minimal owing to the sensitivity of the information concerned. The information that is provided is usually given in aggregate form i.e. totals of foreign debt only.

Table 18   **Disclosure of foreign short-term debt**

	1982–83			
	Large listed	Medium listed	Large unlisted	Total
Number of companies	100	150	50	300
	%	%	%	%
Disclosed totals of UK foreign debt	5	3	–	3
Disclosed loans by currency	–	–	–	–
Disclosed loans by country and continent	1	–	–	–
No foreign debt	1	2	16	4
Not applicable/No information	93	95	84	93
	100	100	100	100

Note: The differences shown in this table, between the disclosures for the three categories of company, are not statistically significant.

However, where there is short-term foreign debt it comprises, on average, 53·56% of total short-term debt as shown in Table 19. Medium listed companies have the highest average percentage at 57·78% but the maximum percentage is to be found in the large listed companies at 86·16%.

79

Table 19   **Foreign short-term debt**

	1982–83			
	Large listed	*Medium listed*	*Large unlisted*	*Total*
Number of companies	6	4	—	10
	%	%	%	%
Mean as a percentage of total short-term debt	50·75	57·78	–	53·56
Minimum	6·17	14·37	–	6·17
Maximum	86·16	84·80	–	86·16

2. Foreign assets

Disclosure of the amount and locations of foreign assets, an important element of risk assessment, is relatively very low with only 20 companies (8%) providing any information in this area (see Table 20). There is a higher level of disclosure by large listed companies relative to medium listed companies. The basis of disclosure, however, is usually by continent or country grouping which may be misleading if major country risks are submerged by other countries in the group.

Table 20   **Disclosure of assets held abroad**

	1982–83			
	Large listed	*Medium listed*	*Large unlisted*	*Total*
Number of companies	*100*	*150*	*50*	*300*
	%	%	%	%
Disclosure of totals of U.K. and foreign assets only	1	–	–	–
Disclosure by country	2	1	–	1
Disclosure by continent or country grouping.......................	12	3	–	6
Not disclosed	83	84	64	80
No evidence of foreign operations (Note 1)	2	12	36	13
	100	100	100	100

Notes:
1. Including one medium-sized company with foreign debt only.
2. The differences shown in this table, between the disclosures for the three categories of listed company, are statistically significant.

3. Qualitative information

As can be seen in Table 21, a relatively large number of company reports (35%) include qualitative comment on the effect of exchange rate changes on performance. However, there is much less comment on matters concerning the likely impact of specific country risks (4%), the effect of exchange rate changes on net borrowings (4%), and the effect on operations of problems in overseas economies (8%) on account of foreign currency shortages, import controls and so on.

While these comments tend to be subjective they may nevertheless provide some useful insights into current performance and future prospects as perceived by Directors.

Table 21   Disclosure of additional qualitative information

| | 1982–83 | | | |
	Large listed	Medium listed	Large unlisted	Total
Number of companies *100*	*100*	*150*	*50*	*300*
	%	%	%	%
Effect of exchange rate changes on performance (i.e. profits and sales)	56	31	8	35
Assessment of specific country risks.....	10	1	2	4
Effect of exchange rate changes on net borrowings........................	6	3	4	4
Effect of problems in overseas economies (e.g. currency shortages, import controls, etc.)	9	9	—	8

Summary and conclusions

Against a background of minimal reporting requirements, the level of disclosure by the large majority of UK companies surveyed is relatively high and is already consistent with much that will be required under SSAP 20. It seems likely that the new accounting standard will be most effective in limiting the variety of treatments in respect of exchange differences, an area of notorious difficulty and potential manipulation, and in requiring more information about the amounts involved. At the same time, SSAP 20 does not go as far as FASB 52 in the USA in terms of disclosure. Neither does SSAP 20 go as far as that minority of companies surveyed which currently disclose the net amount of exchange differences overall which are charged/credited to the profit and loss account and which also provide information about such matters as foreign currency loans and foreign assets. If it is accepted that an evaluation of exchange risks relating to foreign transactions and operations is of major importance in assessing company prospects then further attention to foreign currency accounting issues seems warranted.

EXAMPLES

The accounting policies disclosed by Examples 1 to 3, Imperial Group, Bridon and the Wellcome Foundation, provide some useful examples, in respect of foreign currencies, from the large listed, medium listed and large unlisted company groupings. An interesting and clear analysis of loan capital with special reference to foreign loans is provided by Example 4, Pilkington Brothers. The disclosure of net assets and capital employed by geographical area are the subject of additional information provided by Examples 5 and 6, Inchcape and Dalgety respectively.

Example 1
Imperial Group PLC   *31 October 1982*
Accounting policies:

1 Translation of foreign currencies

Foreign currency assets and liabilities are translated into sterling at the rates ruling on 31st October, except for U.S. dollar borrowings covered forward which are included at the forward cover rate.

Exchange differences arising in the Group's consolidated accounts on the retranslation to closing rates of exchange of its net investments in overseas subsidiaries and associated companies are recorded as movements on the Group's consolidated reserves. Where such net investments are matched in whole or in part by external foreign currency borrowings by the parent company or a U.K. subsidiary, then the exchange differences arising on the retranslation of such matched borrowings are also recorded as movements on the Group's consolidated reserves. Average rates of exchange are used to translate the profit and loss account figures of foreign subsidiaries and associated companies in the consolidated profit and loss account, and differences arising between the translation of these figures at average and closing rates of exchange are recorded as movements on the consolidated reserves.

All other exchange differences are dealt with through the profit and loss account.

Example 2
Bridon PLC   *31 December 1982*
Accounting policies:

(c) Treatment of Foreign Currencies

Assets and liabilities in foreign currencies are translated into sterling at exchange rates ruling at the year end. Trading results of overseas subsidiary and associated companies are translated into sterling at average rates of exchange ruling during the year. Gains and losses arising from the application of these principles are treated as follows:

(i)   gains and losses which arise from trading operations are credited or charged in arriving at the trading profits of the year;

(ii)   gains and losses arising on translation into sterling of the net assets of overseas subsidiaries and associated companies are credited or charged to reserves;

(iii)   gains and losses on long-term foreign currency borrowings are taken to Profit and Loss Account except when borrowings have been used to finance equity investments in the same currency. In this case, gains and losses are offset, as reserve movements, against the exchange differences arising on the investment. This represents a change of accounting policy as set out in Note . ..

Example 3
The Wellcome Foundation Ltd.   *28 August 1982*
Notes to the accounts:

(c) Foreign currencies

(i) All balance sheet items in foreign currencies are translated to sterling at the appropriate rates ruling at 28th August 1982, except that the net book values of fixed assets in certain countries where there is hyper-inflation are translated at the rates ruling at the dates of acquisition. Profit and loss account items in foreign currencies are translated to sterling at the average rates ruling during the financial year.

(ii) No account is taken of the effect of fluctuations in exchange rates occurring after the year end.

(iii) Exchange differences arising on translation of overseas subsidiaries' accounts for consolidation purposes are passed directly through reserves, except those arising in certain countries where there is hyper-inflation, which are reflected in the profit and loss account of the year. All other exchange differences are reflected in the profit and loss account of the year.

Example 4
Pilkington Brothers PLC   *31 March 1983*
Notes to the accounts:

	1981					1982	
Group £m	Company £m					Group £m	Company £m
18 Loan capital							
					Repayable		
9·0	9·0	Sterling		unsecured 15% loan	1982/83	**6·0**	**6·0**
25·0	25·0			unsecured variable rate loans	1983/86	**25·0**	**25·0**
3·4	—			unsecured various	1982/86	**2·0**	**1·6**
·5	—			unsecured various*	1992	**·5**	—
16·1	16·1	U.S.$	36·0m	unsecured 11⅜% loans	1985/87	**20·2**	**20·2**
7·6	7·6		17·1m	unsecured 10⅝% loan	1982	**9·6**	**9·6**
6·7	6·7		15·0m	unsecured 11% loan	1983	**8·4**	**8·4**
2·9	2·9		6·4m	unsecured 9⅞% loans	1984/85	**3·6**	**3·6**
2·2	2·2		11·8m	unsecured variable rate loan	1986	**6·7**	**6·7**
·7	·7		5·5m	unsecured various	1985	**2·8**	**·8**
4·8	—		1·4m	secured various	1982/88	**·8**	—
			93·2m				
17·8	17·8	D.Mk.	84·0m	unsecured 10¼% loan	1986/90	**19·5**	**19·5**
16·9	16·9		80·0m	unsecured variable rate loan	1985/90	**18·6**	**18·6**
8·5	8·5		40·0m	unsecured 9¼% loan	1990	**9·3**	**9·3**
3·1	—		31·7m	unsecured various	1982/95	**7·4**	—
9·6	—		48·5m	secured various	1982/2000	**11·3**	—
			284·2m				
4·1	—	Sw.Kr.	42·3m	secured variable rate loan	1986	**4·0**	—
2·4	—		25·0m	secured variable rate loan*	1982/88	**2·4**	—
2·3	—		17·2m	secured variable rate loan	1982/88	**1·6**	—
4·2	—		40·1m	secured 10¼% bonds	1982/94	**3·8**	—
·5	—		5·5m	unsecured variable rate loan*	1982/91	**·5**	—
1·3	—		12·0m	secured 10½% loan	1982/93	**1·1**	—
4·6	—		37·2m	secured various	1982/98	**3·5**	—
—	—		6·1m	unsecured various	1982/85	**·6**	—
			185·4m				
3·1	—	Nigerian Naira	5·7m	secured variable rate loan	1984/89	**4·7**	—
2·0	—	Aus.$	·9m	secured various	1982/86	**·6**	—
1·2	—		3·4m	unsecured various	1982/85	**2·0**	—
			4–3m				
1·7	—	Other loans		secured		**2·4**	—
3·6	—			unsecured		**·6**	—
165·8	113·4					**179·5**	**129·3**

*also guaranteed by Pilkington Brothers P.L.C.

Supplementary analyses

109·3	79·4	Bank loans	**128·8**	**98·3**
20·0	9·0	Other loans wholly repayable within five years	**34·8**	**31·0**
36·5	25·0	Other loans wholly or partly repayable after five years	**15·9**	—
165·8	113·4		**179·5**	**129·3**
15·5	3·0	Loans due for repayment within one year	**23·5**	**17·6**
22·9	15·6	Loans due for repayment after one year and before two years	**21·4**	**16·4**
44·2	32·2	Loans due for repayment after two years and before five years	**74·0**	**57·3**
83·2	62·6	Loans due for repayment after five years	**60·6**	**38·0**
165·8	113·4		**179·5**	**129·3**

Notes
The Group's foreign currency borrowings, expressed in Sterling, have increased by £16·4 million, and the company's by £14·0 million, as a result of changes in exchange rates during the year. Interest on variable rate loans varies with prevailing interest rates.

Example 5
Inchcape PLC   *31 December 1982*
Report of the Directors:

11. Geographical distribution of net assets

	1982 £000	%	1981 £000	%
United Kingdom	90,685	16	101,974	19
Europe—Continent	16,772	3	13,747	3
Far East	141,040	25	131,962	25
South East Asia	197,440	35	154,934	29
India	5,054	1	4,672	1
Middle East	38,782	7	33,501	6
Africa	9,634	1	18,295	4
The Americas and the Caribbean	34,301	6	39,489	7
Australia and the South Pacific	33,323	6	32,200	6
	567,031	100	530,774	100

Representing:		
Shareholders' capital employed	423,949	407,063
Minority interests	74,299	61,132
Central borrowings	68,783	62,579
	567,031	530,774

Example 6
Dalgety PLC   *30 June 1982*
Analysis of capital employed by area:

	UK £m	Australia £m	New Zealand £m	USA £m	Canada £m	Africa £m	Head Office £m	Total £m
Group funds	178·2	39·7	28·5	55·5	31·2	18·7	(71·6)*	280·2
Minority shareholders' interests	0·6	0·5	19·1	—	—	—	—	20·2
Loan capital	72·0	16·7	13·9	7·2	2·6	—	42·1	154·5
Short-term borrowings	2·9	18·5	20·0	6·9	8·7	—	5·7	62·7
Deferred tax	—	(0·3)	0·3	0·2	—	—	—	0·2
	253·7	75·1	81·8	69·8	42·5	18·7	(23·8)	517·8
Bank balances and deposits	2·5	12·9	0·5	0·4	0·2	5·8	0·1	22·4
Debtors	105·1	28·7	45·1	47·3	19·9	1·6	0·5	248·2
Inventories	110·2	29·8	30·0	36·3	11·0	—	—	217·3
	217·8	71·4	75·6	84·0	31·1	7·4	0·6	487·9
Creditors	128·2	31·0	20·6	46·0	14·6	—	1·3	241·7
Tax	0·6	0·5	0·6	0·2	(0·7)	0·6	8·1	9·9
Dividends proposed and declared	—	—	—	—	—	—	17·2	17·2
	128·8	31·5	21·2	46·2	13·9	0·6	26·6	268·8
Working capital	89·0	39·9	54·4	37·8	17·2	6·8	(26·0)	219·1
Associated companies and investments	3·1	14·3	2·0	3·0	—	10·8	—	33·2
Fixed assets	154·1	19·6	25·2	29·0	23·6	1·1	1·6	254·2
Goodwill	7·5	1·3	0·2	—	1·7	—	0·6	11·3
Total capital employed	253·7	75·1	81·8	69·8	42·5	18·7	(23·8)	517·8
1981	252·7	88·1	80·5	60·6	33·0	16·4	(23·7)	507·6

Notes
Figure for United Kingdom include other European countries.
*The negative figure for Head Office 'group funds' arises from investments in overseas subsidiaries financed by head office loan capital.

84

FURTHER READING

R. Z. Aliber and C. P. Stickney. "Measures of Foreign Exchange Exposure: The long and short of it" *The Accounting Review* (January 1975) pp. 44–57.

J. S. Arpan and Lee H. Radebaugh *International Accounting and Multinational Enterprises* (Warren, Gorham and Lamont, 1981) ch. 5–6.

F. D. S. Choi. "Price – level Adjustments and Foreign Currency Translation: Are they Compatible" *International Journal of Accounting* (Fall 1975) pp. 121–143.

European Economic Community *Seventh Directive on Consolidated Financial Statements* (June 1983).

Financial Accounting Standards Board. Statement of Financial Accounting Standards No. 52. *Foreign Currency Translation* (December 1981).

Flower, John. "Foreign Currency Translation" in Nobes, C. W. and Parker, R. H. (Editors) *Comparative International Accounting* (Philip Allan, 1981) ch. 11.

Institute of Chartered Accountants in England and Wales. Statement of Standard Accounting Practice No. 20. *Foreign Currency Translation* (April 1983).

International Accounting Standards Committee. International Accounting Standard No. 21. *Accounting for the Effects of Changes in Foreign Exchange Rates* (July 1983).

C. W. Nobes. "A Review of the Translation Debate" *Accounting and Business Research* (Autumn 1980) pp. 421–431.

Companies Acts 1948–1981, HMSO, London

GROUP ACCOUNTS

D. M. C. E. Steen and R. M. Wilkins

INTRODUCTION

This section deals with the presentation of and accounting treatment used in group accounts. It includes information disclosed with regard to: exclusion from full consolidation; goodwill; acquisition and disposal of subsidiaries; minority interests; group accounting dates; investments and other interests in subsidiaries in the accounts of holding companies. If group accounts are to be more readily comparable one with another it is important that companies achieve an appropriate measure of consistency in these fundamental areas. In addition where there are material changes in the composition of a group it is important that adequate information regarding the effect of this is disclosed.

REQUIREMENTS

As the different aspects of group accounts considered in this Survey are diverse in nature the various requirements are dealt with by topic rather than by the source of the requirement (i.e. statute, standard accounting practice, EEC Directives, Stock Exchange). What follows is no more than a brief overview of some of the more complex requirements.

Form of group accounts

There is a general statutory requirement for holding companies to present group accounts in the form of a consolidation including all subsidiaries. An alternative form of group accounts to a single consolidation may be presented if it is the directors' opinion that this would better present the same or equivalent information so that it may be readily appreciated by the company's members (1948, Ss. 150 and 151). In addition group accounts need not deal with the accounts of a particular subsidiary if the directors consider that (1948, S. 150):

1. it is impracticable, or would be of no real value because of the insignificant amounts involved, or would involve undue expense or delay; or
2. the result would be misleading or harmful to the business; or
3. the businesses of the companies are so different that they cannot reasonably be treated as a single undertaking.

Any omission on the grounds of being harmful or due to the difference of the business requires the approval of the Department of Trade and Industry.

If a holding company does not submit group accounts or if consolidated accounts are prepared and any subsidiaries are not dealt with therein, additional information should be given, including the reasons for the omission (1948 Sch. 8, 69 and Sch. 8A, 15(4) and 21).

The Companies Act 1981 applies the prescribed formats and other requirements of the new Schedule 8 to group accounts as well as to individual company accounts and this is mandatory for accounting periods starting on or after 15th June 1982. None of the companies in the survey were required to follow the

1981 Act rules but 20 companies (12 large listed, 4 medium listed and 4 large unlisted) adopted them on a voluntary basis.

The EEC 7th Directive, which was adopted on 13th June 1983, has a general requirement for a single set of consolidated accounts. The Directive goes into much greater detail than the present UK law on the subject, but its requirements do not have to be included in national law until 1st January 1988. There are a considerable number of member state options in the Directive and although it will require some changes in the UK, its effect will not be anything like as dramatic as it will be in most of the other EEC countries, where full consolidation has not previously been required.

SSAP 14 "Group Accounts" codifies UK practice in this area and states that only exceptionally will alternative forms of group accounts give a better view than a single set of consolidated accounts including all subsidiaries. SSAP 14 sets out four situations where subsidiaries should be excluded from consolidation (very dissimilar activities, lack of control, severe restrictions on control and temporary control) and specifies the accounting treatment and disclosures to be adopted in each of these cases. Where a subsidiary is excluded from group accounts, consideration will need to be given to whether the resulting accounts give a true and fair view of the position of the group as a whole.

A description of the bases on which subsidiary companies have been dealt with in the group accounts should be given. Uniform accounting policies should be applied in the preparation of consolidated accounts.

Compliance with SSAP 14 (together with SSAP 1 "Accounting for associated companies") will automatically ensure compliance with the International Accounting Standard IAS 3 "Consolidated financial statements".

Table 1 deals with the exclusion of subsidiaries from the main consolidated accounts.

Accounting dates

Statute requires the financial year end of each subsidiary to be the same as that of the holding company unless, in the opinion of the holding company's directors, there are good reasons against it (1948, S. 153(1)), in which case disclosure should be made of the directors' reasons for differing year ends and the accounting dates of the relevant subsidiaries.

The EEC 7th Directive (not yet applicable in the UK) states that where a subsidiary's accounting date is over three months prior to the group accounting date, interim accounts for that subsidiary up to the group accounting date must be used (Article 27(3)).

SSAP 14 requires coterminous dates and periods, wherever practicable, with specified disclosures where there are exceptions to this.

Tables 2 and 3 deal with non-coterminous accounting dates.

Minority interests

There are currently no statutory disclosure requirements for minority interests. The EEC 7th Directive requires separate disclosure of minority interests in the consolidated profit and loss account and balance sheet.

SSAP 14 requires minority interests in the share capital and reserves of subsidiaries to be disclosed separately in the consolidated balance sheet with debit balances only being recognised if there is a binding obligation on the minority to make good losses which they are able to meet. Profits or losses attributable to minorities should be shown separately in the profit and loss account after group profit or loss after tax but before extraordinary items, the latter being shown net of related minority interests.

Table 4 analyses the presentation of minority interests in the profit and loss account.

Changes in the composition of a group

There are no legal requirements specifically covering disclosures in respect of changes in the composition of a group, apart from the special merger relief disclosures introduced in 1982 (discussed below). However where shares are issued at a premium as consideration for an acquisition a share premium account has to be set up except where share premium relief applies, that is where there is either (a) a share for share exchange taking a holding to at least 90% of the acquired company's equity or (b) a qualifying intra-group transfer (1948 S. 56 and 1981 Ss. 36 to 40).

SSAP 14 includes certain requirements (see below) regarding the acquisition and disposal of subsidiaries. The subject of "Accounting for acquisitions and mergers" is dealt with more fully in the ASC Exposure Draft under that title issued in October 1982 (ED 31).

ED 31 proposed methods of accounting for two types of business combination and proposed certain conditions which distinguish them. A combination which meets all the conditions would be accounted for as a merger (pooling of interests); all other combinations would be accounted for as acquisitions. The principal conditions which would have to be met in order that the combination be accounted for as a merger are that (a) no material resources leave the combining companies and (b) the offeror company should acquire at least 90% of the shares in the offeree company. The relative size of the combining companies is not proposed as a condition.

In merger accounting, the shares in the subsidiary are recorded by the holding company at the nominal value of the shares which it issues in exchange, and this can only be applied where share premium relief is available (1981 Ss. 36–40). The financial statements of the parties to the merger would be combined as if they had always been merged (thus involving the restatement of pre-merger figures).

In acquisition accounting, the shares in a subsidiary are recorded at the fair value of the consideration given and goodwill often arises. Acquisition accounting is a well established method of accounting for business combinations and is described in SSAP 14, as referred to below.

SSAP 14 requires that the net tangible and identifiable intangible assets of subsidiaries purchased should be stated at their fair value to the acquiring company. Where such values are not incorporated in the books of the acquired company appropriate adjustments should be made on consolidation. Any differences between the purchase consideration and the fair value attributed to the assets will represent goodwill or negative goodwill arising on consolidation.

SSAP 14 also requires that when subsidiaries are either acquired or sold during the accounting period the "effective date" for accounting purposes should be the earlier of the date when the consideration passes or the offer becomes or is declared unconditional, even if the acquiring company has the right to share in the profits from an earlier date.

In the case of material additions to or disposals from the group, the consolidated financial statements should contain sufficient information about the results of the subsidiaries acquired or sold to enable shareholders to appreciate the effect on the consolidated results. This requirement of SSAP 14 is expressed in very general terms and the SSAP does not give any guidance as to what "sufficient" information is. For example, it does not state whether the effect on turnover, interest, profit before tax and/or other profit and loss account items should be given. Neither does it specify (a) the length of the period following acquisition for which information should be given, (b) whether only the overall impact on the group should be shown, or acquisitions and disposals should be shown separately, or major acquisitions individually if there are several in a year, or (c) whether any pre-acquisition information is relevant (particularly if there is rapid integration following the acquisition making the production of post-acquisition information impracticable). The requirement relates only to the "results", and thus does not cover the impact on the group balance sheet (although para. 7 of SSAP 10 recommends footnotes to the Source and Application of Funds Statement analysing the Balance Sheet impact).

Listed companies are required to send a Class 1 circular to shareholders regarding major acquisitions and disposals, as defined by The Stock Exchange. In the case of disposals, the profit and loss information given in the circular would normally meet the SSAP 14 requirement and to that extent it should be reflected in the presentation of the subsequent annual accounts. The ASC Discussion Paper reviewing SSAP 6 (published in January 1983) recommended that where the effect of discontinued operations is material, then "either the results of continuing businesses or the results of the discontinued operations should be given in the financial statements by way of a note to the profit and loss account" (para. 4.6).

There are additional legal disclosure requirements where Section 37 (1981) (share premium relief) is applicable. These include particulars and the amount of any profit or loss on the disposal of fixed assets (including investments) held by the acquired company (or group) at the time of acquisition, which occurs in the year of acquisition or the following 2 years (S.I. 1982 No. 1092, effective for accounts prepared on or after 1st November 1982).

The EEC 7th Directive requires that where the composition of a group changes significantly, the consolidated accounts must include information which makes the comparison of successive sets of consolidated accounts meaningful (Article 28).

In November 1983, the IASC published IAS 22 "Business Combinations", to be effective from 1st January 1985. IAS 22 deals with acquisition and merger accounting and is generally less restrictive than the proposals in ED 31. One additional disclosure to those in ED 31 where the merger method is used is the amount of assets and liabilities contributed by each party to the merger.

Tables 5 and 6 analyse the disclosures given regarding acquisitions and disposals.

Treatment of goodwill

The rules in the Companies Act 1981 regarding the accounting treatment of goodwill by an individual company do not apply to goodwill arising on consolidation. However it seems that the prescribed formats and the prohibition on offsets may have the effect of barring the so-called "dangling debit" treatment (i.e. the deduction of goodwill from reserves in the balance sheet, where the goodwill is not actually written off but is shown permanently as a deduction from reserves).

The EEC 7th Directive (which as noted must be included in UK law by 1st January 1988) requires that consolidation goodwill must be dealt with in the same way as individual company goodwill under the 4th Directive (i.e. it must be written off within 5 years, but with an option for Member States to extend this to the useful economic life of the item concerned). The immediate write off against reserves is expressly permitted (Article 30).

ED 30 ''Accounting for goodwill'' was published in October 1982. This proposed that all goodwill, including consolidation goodwill, should either be written off on acquisition against reserves representing realised profits or be carried as an asset and amortised against trading profit on a systematic basis over its estimated useful economic life (but not exceeding 20 years). Consolidation goodwill would thus not be able to be carried in a balance sheet as a permanent item. In a Statement of Intent in July 1983 the ASC decided to encourage immediate elimination as the normal accounting practice, but to allow amortisation as an alternative (without stipulating a maximum period of write off; the ASC indicated that it would provide guidance regarding the period over which the amortisation should take place). ED 30 proposed that negative goodwill should be taken to unrealised reserves (from which it may be transferred to realised reserves as the relevant assets are depreciated or sold), unless it represents a provision for future losses and/or costs anticipated at the date of acquisition. Disclosure was proposed for any goodwill (positive or negative) arising in the year, separately for each acquisition.

Table 7 analyses the treatment of goodwill.

Holding company accounts

UK company law requires the presentation of the holding company's own balance sheet, although the holding company profit and loss account need not be presented, subject to specified conditions (1948, Ss. 149(5) and 149A(5)). The additional disclosures required by the 1981 Companies Act should make the holding company balance sheet more informative, although its purpose is largely confined to legal matters, such as solvency and in assessing the extent to which profits are distributable under the 1980 Companies Act (for this purpose the group position is ignored). The 1981 Act will require, inter alia, the following information to be given:–

a) inter-company debtors and creditors analysed into those due in over 1 year and under 1 year,
b) the basis of stating investments in subsidiaries. Any revaluations must either be at market value or directors' value (in which case the method and reasons for adopting it must be disclosed) and the revaluation surplus credited to the separate revaluation reserve,
c) historical cost information for revalued investments.
d) movements during the year on all fixed asset investments (both shares and loans), and
e) amounts written off fixed asset investments shown separately from the gross amount.

The 1948 Act has required a holding company to show in its own accounts as separate items the aggregate amount of shares in subsidiaries and the aggregate amount of indebtedness to and from its subsidiaries (Sch. 8A, 15(2)). The aggregate amount of indebtedness will not necessarily be shown in accounts prepared under the 1981 Act as holding companies are required to disclose shares in and loans to subsidiary companies as a separate classification under fixed assets, all other inter-company indebtedness being classified as either debtors or creditors (1948, Sch. 8, 59). Particulars of each subsidiary are to be shown in the accounts or in a note or statement attached (1967, S. 3).

In addition, SSAP 14 requires the nature of the business of the principal subsidiaries to be disclosed.

For listed companies The Stock Exchange in its "Listing Agreement – Companies" (paragraph 10(d)), requires details to be given of the principal country in which each subsidiary operates: this is additional to disclosure of the country of incorporation required by the Companies Act 1967 (S. 3).

Tables 8 and 9 analyse the disclosure regarding investments in subsidiaries.

ANALYSIS

Exclusion from consolidation

Where subsidiaries were excluded from the main consolidated accounts the reasons were as follows (1981–82 information is not available):–

Table 1   **Subsidiaries excluded from consolidation**

	1982–83			
	Large listed	Medium listed	Large unlisted	Total
Number of companies	*100*	*150*	*50*	*300*
	%	%	%	%
Dissimilar activities	4	2	4	3
Lack of control	2	1	—	1
Severe restrictions	5	—	2	2
Temporary control	1	1	—	1
Impracticable	1	—	—	—
Insignificant........................	—	2	4	2
Subsequent disposal	—	1	—	1
Other (Note 1)	—	—	2	—
	13	7	12	10

Notes:
1. This is related to newly formed overseas subsidiaries for which no accounts were available and where trading was just starting.
2. The differences shown in this table, between the exclusion of subsidiaries from consolidation (irrespective of the reason) by the three categories of company, are not statistically significant.

In most cases the detailed provisions of SSAP 14, which are more restrictive than those of the Companies Acts, were followed, although in some instances the treatment adopted was not entirely clear.

The most common single reason for exclusion from consolidation was *dissimilar activities* and in 7 of the 8 examples of this, the subsidiaries concerned were "exempt" banks or insurance companies where the accounts may be prepared on a fundamentally different basis from those of other companies in the group. In all 7 of these cases the results were consolidated in the profit and loss account in the normal way and a separate balance sheet of these activities was presented. In 6 cases the attributable net assets were included in the main consolidated balance sheet on an equity basis and in 1 case the investment was shown at directors valuation. The 8th example (a large unlisted group) stated the excluded subsidiaries at cost in the group balance sheet and on a dividend basis in the group profit and loss account (whereas SSAP 14 requires the use of the equity method).

The other categories of excluded subsidiaries tended to be of less significance in the context of the overall size of the group concerned and correspondingly less information was normally given.

There were 3 examples of exclusion arising from *lack of control*, including 1 case where there was power to appoint the majority of the Board but where slightly under 50% of the shares were owned (the equity method of accounting was used). In the other 2 cases there was no significant influence (in one case the parent held only a minority of the votes with no representation on the Board, and in the other the subsidiary was in liquidation) and the investments werer carried at cost and nil value respectively.

The countries where *severe restrictions* were encountered included Zimbabwe, Uganda, Argentina, India, Bangladesh and Ethiopia. In 2 of the 6 cases of this, results were included in full, in 2 cases they were included on a remittance basis and in 2 cases they were excluded (1 of which was stated to be immaterial). In all cases some provision had been made against the balance sheet values.

There were 3 examples of *temporary control* and in all cases the controlling shareholding had been purchased during the year with the intention of disposal. One case related to certain subsidiaries within a sub-group acquired. In the other 2 cases a minority holding was being retained.

One example of exclusion through *impracticality* arose and this related to a subsidiary acquired during the year which was stated at cost. The acquisition accounts had not been agreed with the vendor and consequently the results for the post-acquisition period were not obtainable.

There were 2 cases of *subsequent disposal*, in both of which the disposal was completed shortly after the balance sheet date and full details of the effect on the group were given. In one case a material loss on disposal was incurred and full provision made. In the other case a subsidiary was exchanged for an interest in an associate (plus cash) under a conditional pre balance sheet agreement completed after the year-end.

Accounting dates

For large companies the details regarding the bases of consolidation of subsidiaries were often contained in a separate accounting policy note covering such items as the accounting dates of subsidiaries, the treatment of acquisitions and disposals and goodwill arising on consolidation. The information given relating to the accounting dates of subsidiaries consolidated is summarised in Table 2.

Table 2   **Policy relating to accounting dates of subsidiaries**

	1982–83				1981–82
	Large listed	Medium listed	Large unlisted	Total	Total
Number of companies	100	150	50	300	300
	%	%	%	%	%
Different accounting dates used with reasons stated as follows:					
to avoid undue delay	14	8	4	9	11
seasonal nature of trade	2	1	2	1	1
administrative reasons	5	3	2	4	3
immateriality	2	—	—	1	1
other specified reasons	2	4	2	3	3
no reasons given	1	6	—	3	7
	26	22	10	21	26
Co-terminous accounting periods specifically stated	39	54	58	50	47
No specific mention of subsidiary company accounting dates	35	24	28	28	27
No subsidiaries	—	—	4	1	—
	100	100	100	100	100

Note: The differences shown in this table, between the use (for whatever reason) of different accounting dates by subsidiaries of the three categories of company, are not statistically significant.

Table 2 shows that only 28% of the companies made no specific reference to subsidiary company accounting dates, presumably on the basis that co-terminous periods are implied unless a specific statement is made to the contrary.

There were 3 examples (all large listed) of a 15 month period for certain overseas subsidiaries being included in the group results, arising from a change of accounting date to bring it into line with the rest of the group. In two cases the effect was quantified.

Where non-coterminous accounting dates were used, the interval between the subsidiary and group accounting dates is summarised in Table 3.

Table 3 Non-coterminous accounting dates

| | 1982–83 | | | | 1981–82 |
	Large listed	Medium listed	Large unlisted	Total	Total
Number of companies	100	150	50	300	300
	%	%	%	%	%
Interval:–					
1 month	4	5	—	4	
2 months	3	2	—	2	
3 months	10	12	6	10	N/A
4 months	1	—	2	1	
6 months	4	2	2	3	
Unspecified................	4	1	—	2	
	26	22	10	22	26

Note: The differences shown in this table, between the length of interval for subsidiaries of the three categories of company, are not statistically significant.

As noted above the implementation of the EEC 7th Directive will effectively result in a maximum interval of three months. In most cases it is difficult to see why an interval of more than a month should be necessary, at least where the reasons given are to avoid undue delay or administrative factors; the majority of large and complex groups have coterminous dates for all subsidiaries.

Minority interests

A minority interest can theoretically be presented at different levels in the profit and loss account, e.g. before or after taxation, before or after extraordinary items. Perhaps the most useful level of calculation is after taxation but before extraordinary items, as required by SSAP 14. Of the alternatives, the minority figure after extraordinary items combines the ordinary and extraordinary (i.e. non-recurring) elements into one, whilst showing the minority interest at the pre-tax level only has the effect that the taxation figures in the profit and loss account (being net of minorities) would not be consistent with those in the balance sheet (being gross of minorities). Table 4 analyses the presentation adopted.

Table 4   **Presentation and incidence of minority interests in group profit and loss accounts**

	1982–83				1981–82
	Large listed	Medium listed	Large unlisted	Total	Total
Number of companies	100	150	50	300	300
	%	%	%	%	%
Below profit after taxation but before extraordinary items (Note 1)...................	83	59	48	65	65
Below profit after taxation and extraordinary items	2	3	8	4	4
Before the charge for taxation	1	1	2	1	2
	86	63	58	70	71
No mention of minority interest (Note 2)....................	14	37	42	30	29
	100	100	100	100	100

Notes:
1. This includes 1 medium listed company where preference dividends were shown before minority interests.
2. This includes 6 companies where there was no mention of minority interest in the profit and loss account although a minority was disclosed in the consolidated balance sheet; presumably the effect on the profit and loss account was considered immaterial.
3. The differences shown in this table, between the presentation of minority interests for the three categories of company, are not statistically significant. However, the differences between the incidence of minority interests are statistically significant.

The balance sheet presentation of minority interest in the share capital and reserves of subsidiary companies was normally to show them below shareholders' funds, often with long term loans and other deferred liabilities.

Changes in the composition of a group

SSAP 14 only has one disclosure requirement ("sufficient information about the results of subsidiaries acquired or sold to enable shareholders to appreciate the effect on the consolidated results"), as opposed to the accounting treatment, in respect of changes in the composition of groups and that requirement is only expressed in rather general terms. EDs 30 and 31 were issued during the period covered by the Survey but they do not yet appear to have had a major impact on disclosure practices. Tables 5 and 6 set out the position regarding disclosure of acquisitions and disposals by groups. Information for 1981–82 is not available.

Table 5   **Acquisitions and mergers**

	Large listed	Medium listed	Large unlisted	Total
	1982–83			
Number of companies	*100*	*150*	*50*	*300*
	%	%	%	%
Acquisitions during the year referred to in the accounts or directors' report	84	42	42	56
Consideration included shares (Note 1) ..	12	5	2	7
Disclosure regarding effect on results (Note 2)	8	6	2	6
Effective date of major acquisitions disclosed (Note 3)	11	21	18	17
Accounting policy refers to inclusion of results from the effective date of acquisition........................	59	38	20	42

Notes:
1. In at least 10 of the 21 cases (7%) where the consideration included shares it appeared that share premium relief (section 37 Companies Act 1981) was available as over 90% of the shares were acquired, although shares sometimes formed only part of the consideration given. However in only 3 of these cases was section 37 relief utilised and in only 2 was full merger accounting treatment adopted, including the restatement of the pre-merger figures (both were in accounts published several months after the issue of ED 31). In all 3 section 37 relief cases there had been a prior interest in the acquiree (in 2 cases the acquiree had been an associate, in the other case a 64% subsidiary), although ED 31 proposes that a prior holding in excess of 10% should rule out the use of merger accounting (para. 9).

   In neither of the 2 cases where merger accounting was adopted was disclosure made of the fair value of the consideration given by the issuing company (as proposed by ED 31), although one company did disclose the amount by which the share premium account would have increased if acquisition accounting had been used. Other disclosures were given relating to the profits included for the company acquired although in neither case were all the disclosures proposed by ED 31 given.
2. Disclosures of the effect on results (18 examples, 6%) include 5 cases where information was given in the directors' report rather than in the accounts and 6 cases where it was specifically noted that the effect of acquisitions was not material. The disclosures given varied considerably. In 6 cases the post acquisition trading, operating or pre-interest profit of the new subsidiary included in the group results was given; in 3 cases the pre-tax post-acquisition profit or loss; in 1 case the after tax post-acquisition profit; in 1 case the combined effect of acquisitions and disposals on sales and pre-tax profits, and in 1 case the effect on the prior year sales, profits, etc. as if the current year group structure had been effective then (some associates had become subsidiaries and vice versa). It is not known how many of the companies issued separate circulars describing the effects of acquisitions.
3. The disclosure of the effective date of major acquisitions includes 35 (5 large listed, 26 medium listed and 4 large private) cases of disclosure in the directors' report.

97

Table 6   **Disposals**

		1982–83		
	Large listed	*Medium listed*	*Large unlisted*	*Total*
Number of companies	100	150	50	300
	%	%	%	%
Disposals during the year referred to in the accounts or directors' report	52	22	8	30
Disclosure regarding effect on results (Note)	10	2	—	4
Effective date of major disposals disclosed	7	13	—	9
Accounting policy refers to inclusion of results to effective date of disposal	46	22	8	28

Note: The examples (4%) of disclosure regarding the effect on results include 3 cases where the information was given in the directors' report. One case was a demerger with effect from the beginning of the year and the comparative figures showed the sales and pre-interest profit of the demerged activities. In 8 cases the pre-disposal operating result of the subsidiary(s) sold was disclosed; in 1 case the contribution to trading profit in both the year of disposal and the previous year was stated to be not of material significance; in 2 cases the pre-tax result was given; and in the remaining case the prior year group figures were stated as if the current year group structure had been effective then. In 3 cases the pre-disposal sales included were also disclosed. It is not known how many of the companies issued separate circulars describing the effects of the disposals.

It is clear from Tables 5 and 6 that large listed companies are more likely to have acquisitions and disposals than the others (and are more likely to state their policy regarding inclusion of results) and these results are statistically significant.

Tables 5 and 6 indicate that, although there was evidence (generally from the directors' report and source and application of funds statement) that a large proportion of groups (particularly larger groups) had acquisitions (56% of total) and/or disposals (30% of total) in the year, only a relatively small number of these (6% regarding acquisitions and 4% regarding disposals) quantified the "effect on the consolidated results" as required by SSAP 14. No doubt in many cases the effect was immaterial, particularly after taking account of the interest effect where the consideration was cash or loan stock, but there were some cases where the consideration given was significant in relation to the group net assets and therefore some disclosure could have been expected, even if it was only to state specifically that the effect on the results was immaterial (as was done in 7 cases).

The majority of companies that made some disclosure interpreted "effect on the consolidated results" as meaning the effect on trading or operating profits (i.e. before interest), although in other cases alternative or additional information was given, such as the effect on sales, interest, pre-tax profits, etc. In several cases, as noted in the tables, the information was given in the directors' report rather than the accounts, which is where SSAP 14 requires the information to be given. The 1981 Companies Act may lead to greater disclosure on this in the accounts themselves as it requires the analysis of turnover and profits by class of business to be given in the accounts rather than the directors' report.

The timing of a major acquisition or disposal also affects the disclosure. For example if a major acquisition is made shortly before a year end it is unlikely to have a material effect on the group results of that year, but it probably would on those of the following year. One company in the survey with a major acquisition a few weeks before the end of the previous year disclosed the amount of that subsidiary's sales and trading profit for (a) the current year (b) the post-acquisition part of the previous year and (c) the whole of the previous year.

Where an acquisition is integrated into an existing business it may be difficult to quantify the effect on the results. One company in the survey noted that an acquisition late in the previous year had substantially benefited the group profit for the current year but as the business had been completely absorbed within the existing businesses the amount could not be separately quantified.

From the statements made in directors' reports it appears that many companies regard the purchase of new subsidiaries (particularly when they are relatively minor acquisitions) as being part of their capital expenditure on fixed assets and the amounts and the effect on the group results were not separately distinguished.

As referred to in Note 1 of Table 5 above, there were only 2 instances of the application of merger accounting, although ED 31 was issued early in the Survey period and had been foreshadowed in the parliamentary debates on the 1981 Companies Act. It was not clear how many business combinations by companies in the Survey met the criteria for a merger proposed by ED 31, but it is interesting to recall that, although ED 3 (also entitled "Accounting for acquisitions and mergers" and issued in 1971) proposed merger accounting for certain share-for-share combinations, the Surveys for 1971-72, 1972-73 and 1973-74 did not identify a single instance of the use of merger accounting, although prior to the issue of ED 3 there had been a number of instances of either the full or partial use of merger accounting.

No instance was noted of the merger disclosures required by S.I. 1982 No. 1092 in relation to accounts dated after 1st November 1982 in cases where share premium relief was available and there had been disposals of fixed assets.

Only 17 companies disclosed in the accounts the actual dates from which the results of major acquisitions had been brought in, as proposed by ED 31, although more often (35 companies) this was given in the directors' report. There is no equivalent requirement or proposal for disclosure of the date of major disposals although 26 companies did give this (the majority again being in the directors' report rather than the accounts).

Treatment of goodwill

The policy adopted for the treatment of consolidation goodwill is set out in Table 7.

Table 7   **Treatment of consolidation goodwill**

| | 1982–83 | | | | 1981–82 |
	Large listed	Medium listed	Large unlisted	Total	Total
Number of companies	*100*	*150*	*50*	*300*	*300*
	%	%	%	%	%
Eliminated immediately against reserves	66	46	32	50	46
Permanent deduction from reserves (dangling debit)	4	4	4	4	1
Written off as an extraordinary item in year of acquisition ...	4	11	18	·10	13
Shown as separate asset amortised through:					
Reserves	—	1	2	1	1
Extraordinary items	2	—	2	1	3
Pre-tax profits ....,.....	2	1	—	1	2
Shown as separate asset not regularly amortised	10	7	10	9	10
	88	70	68	76	76
No goodwill shown	12	30	32	24	24
	100	100	100	100	100
Goodwill shown as arising in the year:–					
Positive goodwill	67	22	20	37	N/A
Negative goodwill	5	9	8	7	
	72	31	28	44	

Note: The differences shown in this table, between the treatment of consolidated goodwill as an asset (whether amortised or not) by the three categories of company, are not statistically significant.

There has been a continuing trend towards the policy of immediate elimination of goodwill against reserves and of the 20 companies (11 large listed, 7 medium listed and 2 large unlisted) which changed their policy on goodwill in the year under review 17 of these were to this basis. In the first Survey, in 1968–69, 124 of the 300 companies treated goodwill as an asset, compared with only 34 in the present Survey.

ED 30 proposed certain disclosures regarding goodwill. All of the 9 companies which amortised goodwill disclosed the maximum period of amortisation (1:8 years; 1:10 years; 3:20 years; 1: major acquisitions over 30 years; 3:40 years); 2 of these companies disclosed all the movements for the year and

2 the charge to profit and loss account. None disclosed the directors' reasons for selecting the number of years over which amortisation is taking place. No instances were noted of a provision for future losses and/or costs being set up out of negative goodwill arising on an acquisition in the period (para. 66 of ED 30), although 1 company referred to this as being its accounting policy. In only 1 case was goodwill analysed between acquisitions (as proposed by para. 67 of ED 30), but in a number of cases it was reasonably clear that there was only one acquisition in the year.

Investments and other interests in subsidiaries in the accounts of holding companies

The various methods of disclosing the division between investment in shares and inter-group indebtedness are summarised in Table 8.

Table 8   Disclosure of investments in shares and amounts owing to and by subsidiaries

	1982–83				1981–82
	Large listed	Medium listed	Large unlisted	Total	Total
Number of companies	100	150	50	300	300
	%	%	%	%	%
Shares and all indebtedness shown together and under a separate assets classification	67	82	64	74	85
Dividends receivable from subsidiaries shown separately as a current asset with all other balances shown together	7	4	4	5	3
Long-term advances with shares, leaving current indebtedness in current assets or current liabilities	21	8	10	13	2
All inter-company indebtedness under current assets or current liabilities	4	6	18	7	10
No subsidiaries	1	—	4	1	—
	100	100	100	100	100

Note: The differences shown in this table, between disclosure practices of companies with subsidiaries for the three categories of company, are statistically significant.

The trend towards an analysis being made of indebtedness between long-term and current (up from 2% to 13% of all companies) may be partly due to the

Companies Act 1981, which requires all assets to be designated as either fixed or current and all creditors to be designated as due either within one year or after more than one year. (20 companies – 12 large listed, 4 medium listed and 4 large unlisted – followed the new 8th Schedule.)

Until the 1981 Act there were no specific regulations controlling the bases of valuation of shares in subsidiaries or the information which should be disclosed in accounts relating thereto. This is reflected in the variety of methods used by the companies in the Survey as set out in Table 9.

Table 9   **Bases of valuation of shares in subsidiaries**

	1982–83				1981–82
	Large listed	*Medium listed*	*Large unlisted*	*Total*	*Total*
Number of companies	*100*	*150*	*50*	*300*	*300*
	%	%	%	%	%
At cost	16	23	30	22	23
At cost less amounts written off	53	49	42	49	52
At current net asset value (Note 1)...................	11	7	6	8	7
At directors' valuation (Note 2)	10	11	12	11	7
Described only as "Shares" (Note 3)...................	5	8	4	6	5
Other (Note 4)	4	2	2	3	6
No subsidiaries	1	—	4	1	—
	100	100	100	100	100

Notes:
1. This is effectively the equity method of valuation, but excluding any premium paid (or discount) on acquisition.
2. Includes some subsidiaries at valuations made in earlier years.
3. Includes "shares less provisions".
4. Includes (a) "at cost plus surpluses on certain revaluations of properties less amounts written off"; (b) "net assets at date of acquisition"; (c) "at cost or at book value of net assets on acquisition less provision"; (d) "book values equivalent to issued share capitals and unrealised reserves less appropriate provisions"; and (e) "at net assets acquired or at cost".
5. The differences shown in this table, between the bases of valuation of shares for the three categories of company, are not statistically significant.

As last year, all companies in the Survey gave details of either all or their principal subsidiaries, and in most cases this information was shown in a separate statement. Frequently this statement was separated from the main part of the accounts by additional non-statutory information but in all except 18 (4 large listed, 12 medium listed and 2 large unlisted) cases (1981–82: 34) there was either a cross reference from the main part of the accounts or the audit report made it clear that the separate statement was part of the accounts.

In 57 (18 large listed, 30 medium listed and 9 large unlisted) instances (1981–82: 93) it was not made clear which shares were held directly by the holding company and which were held by subsidiaries, as required by section 3 of the Companies Act 1967.

In 108 (27 large listed, 53 medium listed and 28 large unlisted) instances, (1981–82 not available) an indication of the nature of the business of the principal subsidiaries was not disclosed in the group accounts, as required by paragraph 33 of SSAP 14, although this information was sometimes found elsewhere in the report, such as the review of operations. In some cases the Directors' Report noted or implied that only one class of business was carried on by the group.

Amongst companies categorised as listed 78 (37 large, 41 medium) out of 250 (1981–82: 132 out of 300) did not specifically show the principal country of operation of subsidiaries, as required by paragraph 10(d) of The Stock Exchange Listing Agreement, but the information could sometimes be implied from the review of operations. The majority of companies complying with the requirement dealt with it by a simple statement noting that all subsidiaries operated principally in their countries of incorporation.

EXAMPLES

The following examples from the accounts of large listed companies are amongst the more informative illustrations of some of the major matters discussed in this section. Example 1 is a detailed accounting policy note on the principles of consolidation. Example 2 is an accounting policy note on the acquisition and disposal of subsidiaries, including the treatment of goodwill. Example 3 is an accounting policy note that covers the accounting dates of subsidiaries and the policy when shares are issued as consideration for acquisitions. Example 4 shows the effect on group results of a subsidiary acquired during the previous year. Example 5 shows the effect on group results of a subsidiary acquired in the current year; this company also took advantage of section 37 of the Companies Act 1981 and credited the premium on the shares issued as consideration for the acquisition to a reserve other than share premium account. Example 6 illustrates the effect on group results of a disposal during the year.

Other examples of group accounts which readers may find of interest include the following:

(a) The Rio Tinto-Zinc Corporation PLC. This has an additional presentation of the group accounts on what is described as the "proportional equity consolidation" method. This shows the attributable interest of RTZ shareholders in each of the items comprised in the conventional consolidation. The two main differences compared with the conventional consolidation are that the interests of outside shareholders are eliminated against each item and the principal associated companies are dealt with on the same basis as subsidiary companies. A feature of this method is that when an interest in a company changes from say a 49% associate to a 51% subsidiary or vice versa, the impact on the consolidated accounts is only minor.

(b) The 2 examples referred to in the text where merger accounting was adopted were (i) S. Pearson & Son plc – 31st December 1982 – in respect of the acquisition of the 36% minority interest in Pearson Longman plc and (ii) European Ferries plc – 31st December 1982 – in respect of the acquisition of Gakopa NV.

Example 1
Pilkington Brothers P.L.C.   *31 March 1982*
Extract from accounting policies:

9 Group consolidation

The Group accounts consolidate the accounts of Pilkington Brothers P.L.C. and of its subsidiary companies. Where appropriate, the accounts of overseas subsidiary companies are adjusted to conform with the Group's accounting policies.

Any difference between the cost of acquisition of a subsidiary company and its net assets is taken to reserves in the year of the acquisition.

Sales to outside customers include sales by the Group to related companies, but exclude sales by those companies.

The total results of subsidiary companies are included with those of Pilkington Brothers P.L.C. in the Group's profit before and after taxation. Unrealised profits on inter-company transactions are eliminated on consolidation. The proportion of the year's results applicable to minority shareholders in subsidiary companies, and to any pre-acquisition period, is excluded in arriving at the profit attributable to shareholders of Pilkington Brothers P.L.C.

The total assets and liabilities of subsidiary companies are included with those of Pilkington Brothers P.L.C. in the Group balance sheet. Inter-company balances are eliminated on consolidation.

Example 2
Cadbury Schweppes Public Limited Company   *31 December 1982*
Extract from accounting policies:

Acquisition and disposal of subsidiaries

Results of subsidiary companies acquired during the financial year are included in Group profit from the effective date of acquisition and those of companies disposed of up to the effective date of disposal. For this purpose the net tangible assets of newly acquired subsidiaries are incorporated into the accounts on the basis of the fair value to the Group as at the effective date of acquisition. Land and buildings are included at values confirmed by professional valuers.

Any excess of the consideration over the fair value of the net tangible assets of newly acquired subsidiaries at the effective date of acquisition is deducted from reserves on consolidation.

The difference between the sales proceeds and the net assets at the effective date of disposal is taken to profit and loss account.

Example 3
The Great Universal Stores p.l.c.   *31 March 1982*
Extract from accounting policies:

(b) Consolidation of subsidiaries

All subsidiaries make up accounts to 31st March and profits for the twelve months ended on that date are included in the group results in full, except where subsidiaries are acquired during the year when profits are included from the date of acquisition. The profits of subsidiaries sold during the year are included in the group consolidation up to the date of disposal.

When shares have been issued in respect of acquisitions the share premium is computed on the basis of the market value of the shares of The Great Universal Stores p.l.c. at the date of acquisition.

Goodwill relating to newly acquired subsidiaries is written off as an extraordinary item in the consolidated profit and loss account.

Example 4
Brook Bond Group plc   *30 June 1982*
Notes on the accounts:–

3 Mallinson-Denny group
The first full year contribution from Mallinson-Denny, acquired in January 1981, was as follows:–

	1982	1981
		(5 months)
	£000	£000
Trading profit		
United Kingdom & Ireland	**3,799**	2,643
Europe	**(419)**	24
North America	**1,688**	699
Australia	**2,007**	763
Asia	**1,062**	1,364
	8,137	5,493
Interest	**(9,009)**	(3,128)
Profit before tax attributable to Mallinson-Denny	**(872)**	2,365
Group interest charges arising from cash cost of acquisition	**(6,000)**	(3,390)
Dividends	**—**	461
Effect of Mallinson-Denny on group profit before tax	**(6,872)**	(564)

Example 5
S. & W. Berisford PLC   *30 September 1982*
Notes on the accounts:

2. British Sugar plc
From 30th July 1982, the effective date of acquisition of British Sugar as a subsidiary, the contribution to the group profit before interest was £13,458,000.

Example 6
Babcock International plc   *2 January 1983*
Extract from consolidated profit and loss account:

	1982	1981
	£000	£000
Trading profit/(loss)		
Continuing operations	**32,773**	30,356
Discontinued operations	**(4,345)**	(2,793)
	28,428	27,563

Extract from note on trading profit:

The trading loss of discontinued operations includes a loss of £3,963,000 in respect of the nine months' trading to 30th September 1982 of the construction equipment companies disposed of with effect from that date.

FURTHER READING

Wilkins, R.M., *"Group Accounts – the fundamental principles, form and content"*, 2nd Edition, ICAEW, 1979.

Wilkins, R.M., *"An Accountants Digest Guide to Accounting Standards – Group Accounts"*, Accountants Digest No. 69, ICAEW 1978.

Additional references on these subjects can be found in the reading lists "Consolidated accounts" and "Goodwill" available from the Library of the Institute of Chartered Accountants in England and Wales.

PENSION COSTS

C. J. Napier

INTRODUCTION

Disclosure in employers' financial statements of information concerning employees' pensions has become increasingly important with the expansion of private occupational pensions schemes and the rising levels of contribution to such schemes made necessary by improving pension benefits and by the impact of inflation.

The purpose of pension provision is simple: to accumulate sums during the working lives of employees which may be used to pay benefits to the employees when they retire or leave service, and to their dependents after the employees die. The amounts accumulated are intended to secure the benefits so far as possible against the employer's inability to meet his pension promises. In the United Kingdom, the normal method of pension provision is through "funding": the employer, and often employees as well, make regular contributions to a pension scheme legally separate from the employer, and usually administered by trustees.

The determination of the level of contribution required is, however, a highly complex procedure. Given the average period between employees' current service and their ultimate receipt of pension benefits, it is necessary to make assumptions about a large number of significant variables over a considerable time span. The main assumptions fall into two groups: "demographic" assumptions, including the number of employees, their age and sex distribution, and their life expectancy; and "economic" assumptions, such as future salary patterns, the return on the pension scheme's assets, future inflation, and future changes in benefit. The actuaries who advise employers and pension scheme managers are usually able to make demographic assumptions with a high degree of precision; the economic assumptions can seldom be better than intelligent guesses.

Given an estimate of the expected pension benefits, there are several methods recognised by actuaries for determining the pattern of normal contributions to the employer's pension scheme so as to accumulate a sufficient amount to meet the expected benefits when they fall due. Employers usually measure the cost of pension provision in any period in terms of the contributions which they make to their pension scheme in that period. Because of the range of methods for determining their contribution, it is not obvious that the amount contributed is the most appropriate measure, within an accrual accounting framework, of the cost of pension provision.

The accounting problem is complicated by the issues arising when "past service credits" are granted, so that certain employees are promised benefits based on a longer period than their remaining service to retirement; when the current value of the pension scheme's assets is less than that projected when the pattern of contributions was determined; and when the actuary's assumptions determining the employer's normal contributions have to be changed. In these circumstances, the present value of accrued future benefits will generally exceed the value of the pension scheme's assets and a deficit, or "actuarial liability", will exist which the employer must fund through making special contributions to his pension scheme. Such liabilities may themselves be computed on a number of

107

bases, which may or may not take into account expected future salary levels and the position should the employer discontinue supporting his pension scheme. Although there is some question whether such liabilities should be included in the employer's balance sheet, their existence and amount are likely in any event to be significant information to users of employers' financial statements.

Pension cost, whether represented by normal or special contributions, is a significant component of the employer's total employee costs, and one subject to particular problems of measurement and uncertainty. Company law now requires most companies to disclose pension costs and commitments in their financial statements. The Accounting Standards Committee has been considering the treatment of pension costs for some time, and has published an Exposure Draft "Disclosure of Pension Information in Company Accounts" (ED 32). Work continues on the more difficult problem of accounting for pension costs, and the ICAEW has recently published a research study "Accounting for the Cost of Pensions".

REQUIREMENTS

Statutory requirements

Schedule 8 to the Companies Act 1948 now requires companies to disclose any provisions for pensions on their balance sheet under the heading of "Provisions for Liabilities and Charges". In addition, Para. 50 of Schedule 8 specifies that details should be given of any pension commitments, whether provision is made on the balance sheet or not.

Para. 56 of Schedule 8 requires companies to disclose their aggregate staff costs, broken down into wages and salaries, social security costs incurred on behalf of employees, and other pension costs. "Pension costs" are defined in Para. 93 of Schedule 8 as including "any other contributions by the company for the purposes of any pension scheme established for the purpose of providing pensions for persons employed by the company, any sums set aside for that purpose and any amounts paid by the company in respect of pensions without first being so set aside". The Companies Act 1981 exempts "small" companies from disclosing this information.

The Companies Acts also contain detailed disclosure requirements concerning directors' pensions; these are not analysed below.

Standard accounting practice

Until the publication of ED 32 "Accounting for Pension Information in Company Accounts" in May 1983, the main official pronouncement on the disclosure of pension information by employers was an Accounting Recommendation on Retirement Benefits issued by the ICAEW in 1960. The main recommendation covered disclosure in the employers' financial statements of any special contributions in respect of past service credits or to make good a deficiency; routine disclosure of normal pension costs and commitments was not, however, specifically recommended.

ED 32 proposes that "disclosure should be made in financial statements of sufficient information concerning pension arrangements to enable users of the statements to gain a broad understanding of the significance of pension costs in the accounting period and of actual and contingent liabilities and commitments at the balance sheet date". The Exposure Draft lists several specific disclosures, which are summarised below:

(a) the nature and funding of the pension schemes, and any legal obligations of the company;
(b) the accounting policy used for allocating pension costs to accounting periods, and the funding policy if this is different from the accounting policy;
(c) whether pension costs and liabilities are assessed in accordance with the advice of a professionally qualified actuary, and, if so, the date of the most recent actuarial valuation;
(d) the amount charged in the profit and loss account for pension costs, distinguishing between normal charges related to employees' pay and service in the accounting period and other charges or credits;
(e) any commitments to change the rate of contributions or to make special contributions;
(f) any provisions or prepayments in the balance sheet resulting from a difference between accounting and funding policies;
(g) any deficiency on a discontinuance actuarial valuation or on the requirements of the Occupational Pensions Board;
(h) any material investment by the employer's pension schemes in securities of, or assets used by, the employer;
(i) any provision for internally financed pension schemes and any identifiable fund of assets representing the provision;
(j) significant effects in future financial statements of changes in the employer's pension provision.

The disclosures may be modified to deal with employees paid abroad and to summarise the information in the case of individual companies or groups with a number of different pension schemes.

International standards

In January 1983, the IASC issued IAS 19 "Accounting for Retirement Benefits in the Financial Statements of Employers". This requires the disclosure of much the same information as ED 32, but goes further in covering accounting methods. The main requirements in this area are that normal pension costs should be charged to profit and loss account systematically over the expected remaining working lives of the employees covered by the pension scheme and that past service costs should be charged as they arise or allocated systematically over a period not exceeding the expected remaining working lives of the employees affected. IAS 19 limits the actuarial methods which may be used for determining costs by excluding the "pay-as-you-go" and "terminal funding" methods. (Thse methods are rarely found in practice in the United Kingdom outside the public sector.)

Accounting requirements in the United States are covered by SFAS 36 "Disclosure of Pension Information". However, the FASB has been actively examining accounting for pension costs, having issued a Discussion Memorandum on the problem in February 1981, which has been fôllowed by a statement of preliminary views in November 1982. The latter document proposes that one specified actuarial method should be used for determining normal pension costs, even if the employer actually uses another method for funding purposes. This method, referred to as the "projected unit credit" method, is not in common use in the United Kingdom.

Number of items disclosed

This year, 135 companies in the sample disclosed at least one item of pensions-related information (1981-82: 141). Companies usually made this disclosure in their statement of accounting policies and in their notes to the accounts, although 12 companies discussed pensions (often at some length) in the chairman's statement, directors' report, employment report or a separate statement regarding their pension arrangements. Table 1 shows the distribution of companies by the number of pension items disclosed. Over two thirds of the large listed companies in the sample disclosed at least one pension item, while only one third of the medium listed companies and one quarter of the large unlisted companies did so. The differences between these proportions are statistically significant, and it may be concluded that large listed companies are more likely to disclose at least one item of pension information than medium listed and large unlisted companies.

Table 1   **Number of pension items disclosed**

	1982–83				1981–82
	Large listed	*Medium listed*	*Large unlisted*	*Total*	*Total*
Number of companies	*100*	*150*	*50*	*300*	*300*
	%	%	%	%	%
No disclosure	32	63	76	55	53
1–5 items	45	26	22	32	31
6–10 items	22	11	2	13	14
Over 10 items	1	—	—	—	2
	100	100	100	100	100
Mean number of items for companies making any disclosures	4·46	4·29	3·00	4·26	4·33

Note: The differences shown in the table, between the levels of disclosure for the three different categories of company, are statistically significant.

Of those companies disclosing at least one item of pensions-related information, the mean number of items disclosed was 4·26. This is not significantly different from the equivalent mean number of items disclosed for 1981–82 of 4·33. The difference between the mean number of items disclosed by the large listed companies and the medium listed companies is not statistically significant, although the equivalent difference between the means for the medium listed and large unlisted companies is significant. This implies that listed companies are likely to disclose more items of pensions-related information than unlisted companies. However, of those listed companies making pension disclosures, large companies are likely on average to disclose the same number of items as medium companies. Further analysis of the large and medium listed companies in the sample was carried out. It did not reveal any statistically significant relationship between the number of pension items disclosed and company size measured in terms of both turnover and historical cost asset value.

Accounting policies

78 companies (1981–82: 65) referred to pensions in their disclosure of accounting policies. Large listed companies were more likely to do so than medium listed or large unlisted companies. Of these 78 companies, 36 also disclosed quantitative pensions information (such as pension costs or provisions) in their financial statements. In addition, 43 companies disclosed quantitative information without stating an accounting policy for pensions. Thus 79 companies in total included numerical pensions information in their financial statements (1981–82: 83), usually by way of notes to the accounts.

Table 2 **Disclosure of accounting policies on pensions**

| | 1982-83 | | | |
	Large listed	Medium listed	Large unlisted	Total
Number of companies	100	150	50	300
	%	%	%	%
Nature of schemes (e.g. defined benefit or defined contribution).............	1	2	—	1
Externally funded or internally financed	22	14	16	17
Legal obligations of company	1	—	—	1
Accounting policy on costs	27	13	10	17
Funding policy	22	13	10	15
Use of actuary......................	35	15	10	21

Note: Comparative figures for 1981–82 are not available.

Table 2 summarises the main items included in the disclosure of accounting policies for pensions. 52 companies disclosed an accounting policy on pension costs and 46 disclosed their funding policy. In all cases, the funding policy disclosed was to make contributions to the company's pension funds in accordance with actuarial advice. The particular approach used by the actuary in arriving at his funding recommendations was not disclosed. The accounting policy on costs did not generally distinguish between normal and special pension costs, usually stating merely that contributions to pension funds were charged to profit and loss account as incurred. 13 companies disclosed their accounting policy in respect of special contributions arising, for example, from deficiencies on an actuarial valuation and from the granting of past service credits. 5 of these provided in full for the present value of future special contributions, even if these were to be paid over a number of years. The other 8 charged the special contributions to profit and loss account as they fell due for payment.

111

Pension expense

Table 3 analyses the disclosure of pension expense. 29 companies in the sample had chosen to prepare their financial statements so as to disclose the information now required by the Companies Act 1948, and thus disclosed total pension costs. Only a further 29 companies had chosen voluntarily to disclose any component of pension costs: 10 of these showed only special contributions (following the 1960 ICAEW Accounting Recommendation on Retirement Benefits).

Table 3 **Disclosure of pension expense**

| | 1982–83 | | | |
	Large listed	Medium listed	Large unlisted	Total
Number of companies	*100*	*150*	*50*	*300*
	%	%	%	%
Normal and special costs disclosed separately	1	1	—	1
Total cost only disclosed	20	14	8	15
Special cost only disclosed	3	2	8	3
No cost disclosed	76	83	84	81
	100	100	100	100

Notes:
1. Comparative figures for 1981–82 are not available.
2. The differences shown in this table, between the disclosure practices of the three categories of company, are not statistically significant.

For those companies disclosing both total pension expense and total staff costs, pension expense represented on average 8·8% of staff costs for the large listed companies, 4·5% for the medium listed companies, and 5·8% for the large unlisted companies. Although these percentages suggest that pension provision is a greater component of the employee remuneration package for larger than for smaller companies, the differences between them are not statistically significant. This probably reflects the small number of companies – 31 – disclosing both total pension expense and total staff costs, and the range of values – from 2·0% to 16·3% – taken by the ratio of pension expense to total staff costs.

Actuarial involvement

In addition to the 62 companies referring to the use of actuaries in their accounting policy on pensions, a further 24 companies mention elsewhere that actuaries are involved in their pension arrangements. Table 4 shows in more detail the disclosure of information concerning actuarial involvement.

Table 4   **Disclosures concerning actuarial involvement**

| | 1982–83 | | | | 1981–82 |
	Large listed	Medium listed	Large unlisted	Total	Total
Number of companies	100	150	50	300	300
	%	%	%	%	%
Use of actuary	47	22	10	29	30
Frequency of valuation	22	8	—	11	10
Date of most recent valuation	19	10	4	12	11
Result of most recent valuation	22	14	4	15	13

Table 5 analyses the result of the most recent valuation for those companies making this disclosure.

Table 5   **Result of actuarial valuation**

| | 1981–83 | | | |
	Large listed	Medium listed	Large unlisted	Total
Number of companies	22	21	2	45
	%	%	%	%
Basis of valuation given	55	39	—	44
Basis of valuation not given	45	61	100	56
	100	100	100	100
Pension funds in surplus...............	32	9	50	22
Pension funds in deficit	14	9	—	11
Funds in balance or result not clearly stated	54	82	50	67
	100	100	100	100

Notes:
1. Comparative figures for 1981–82 are not available.
2. The differences shown in these tables, between the disclosure practices (and the results of valuation) for the three different categories of company, are not statistically significant.

3 of the 10 companies with funds in surplus disclosed the amount of the surplus. 3 of the 5 companies with funds in deficit disclosed the amount of the deficit; 2 of these arose in relation to the pension funds of overseas subsidiaries.

Despite the evidence of Table 5, we are unable to conclude that the problem of deficits is not a serious one for UK pension schemes. It might be the case for many companies that their pension schemes are being valued by actuaries on a relatively "weak" basis (for example, by failing to take into account future pay increases up to employees' normal retirement dates), so that a statement of solvency or even of surplus could be misleading. Moreover, a substantial number of companies which are likely to have pension schemes make no disclosure in their financial statements as to the position of their schemes: some of these could be in deficit on an actuarial valuation.

Miscellaneous disclosures

ED 32 requires the disclosure of any provisions or prepayments in the employer's balance sheet resulting from differences between the accounting and funding policy and of provisions in respect of internally financed schemes. Table 6 sets out such disclosures.

Table 6   **Disclosure of pension provisions**

	1982–83			
	Large listed	Medium listed	Large unlisted	Total
Number of companies	22	5	—	27
	%	%	%	%
Internally financed scheme	40	80	—	48
Difference between accounting and funding...........................	23	20	—	22
Unspecified	37	—	—	30
	100	100	—	100

Notes:
1. Comparative figures for 1981–82 are not available.
2. The differences shown in this table, between the disclosures for the three categories of company, are not statistically significant.

The provisions in respect of internally financed pension schemes almost invariably related to overseas subsidiaries, where local pension practice frequently involves the making of internal provisions for pensions rather than external funding. Provisions arising as a result of differences between accounting and funding policies were generally a consequence of the immediate provision in the accounts for past service liabilities which were being funded over a number of years. There was no evidence that any company in the sample recorded a normal cost of pension provision in a period which differed from the normal amount funded in that period.

ED 32 also requires disclosure of any material "self-investment" (such as investment by the pension scheme in securities of the employer). 2 companies referred to self-investment, both making negative statements. These indicated that it was the policy of their pension schemes not to invest in the securities of, or lend money to, the employers concerned. No company specifically disclosed any self-investment by its pension schemes as such, but there were 12 instances where the existence of self-investment could be deduced from the disclosure of directors' and other substantial share interests.

EXAMPLES

The first example (United Biscuits (Holdings) plc) is an illustration of accounting policy disclosure for pensions. Ths example describes the treatment of pension costs in somewhat greater detail than do most companies, but the reference to funding and the involvement of actuaries is typical.

EXAMPLE 1
United Biscuits (Holdings plc   *1 January 1983*

Pensions
Pensions relating to current and past service are funded by way of annual contributions to pension plans. The amounts of such contributions are determined following consultation with independent actuaries.

Pension costs are accounted for as follows:

(i)   Contributions in respect of current service, amortisation of past service liabilities (other than those described in (ii) below) and notional interest on unfunded past service liabilities, are charged annually against trading profit.

(ii)   The present value of future contributions relating to unfunded past service liabilities is either accrued and charged to the profit and loss account as an extraordinary item at the time of inception of a pension plan, or where appropriate, accrued by way of adjustment to goodwill at the date of acquisition of a subsidiary.

The second example (Allied-Lyons plc) illustrates the disclosure of detailed pension information made by a few companies. In this example, the disclosure is by way of a note to the accounts. Some other companies (notably Crown House plc and Macarthys Pharmaceuticals plc) provide separate statements regarding their pension arrangements, often including summary accounts for their pension schemes.

Example 2
Allied-Lyons plc   *5 March 1983*

**27. Pension scheme contributions and provisions for retirement benefits.
United Kingdom**
The Group pension schemes are contracted out of the State graduated pension arrangements and, in respect of service from April 1978, benefits are fixed by reference to final pay. There are 51,000 current members, 16,400 pensioners and 14,000 former employees with deferred pension rights. Following the acquisition of J. Lyons & Company Limited it was decided to amend the pension arrangements throughout the group. The new combined pension schemes were introduced on 6th April 1980. The first valuation

will deal with the period to 5th April 1982. The collection of the necessary data for the actuary covering the large number of individuals involved has taken longer than expected. The report is unlikely to be available before the end of July 1983. Valuations of the Allied fund had been carried out annually and the Lyons fund was valued prior to becoming part of the Allied-Lyons fund. On the basis that current contributions continue to apply the actuarial valuations in 1980 indicated that both funds were almost exactly in balance. There is no reason to believe that there will be any significant adjustment required to the level of the company contribution, other than to deal with such matters as increases to pensions since 1980 in excess of the three per cent per annum provided for in the funding of the schemes.

Contributions during the year	**1983**		1982	
	£m	**£m**	£m	£m
Employees		**8·7**		8·6
The group—				
for current service—charged to profit and loss account	**28·5**		27·6	
for past service—charged to provision for retirement benefits	**5·9**	**34·4**	6·1	33·7
		43·1		42·3

This past service charge will continue for another five years and is estimated to exhaust the provision over that time.

Other countries
Group contributions to schemes for employees in other countries totalled £6·4 million (£4·3 million) including £0·1 million (£0·9 million) charged to provisions for retirement benefits.

Provisions for retirement benefits	1983	1982
	£m	£m
Balance 6th March 1982	**19·1**	22·5
Prior year adjustment	**0·3**	—
Currency translation adjustment	**0·1**	0·1
Payments during the year less tax	**(3·0)**	(3·5)
Balance 5th March 1983	**16·5**	19·1

FURTHER READING

Napier, C.J., *Accounting for the Cost of Pensions* (ICAEW, 1983).
Archibald, T. Ross, *Accounting for Pension Costs and Liabilities* (Canadian Institute of Chartered Accountants, 1980).
FASB, *Employers' Accounting for Pensions and Other Postemployment Benefits – Preliminary Views* (FASB, 1982).
Young, M. and Buchanan, N., *Accounting for Pensions* (Woodhead-Faulkner, 1982).

POLITICAL AND CHARITABLE CONTRIBUTIONS

C. J. Cowton

INTRODUCTION

One of the statutory disclosure provisions faced by companies in the UK is the requirement to reveal the level of their payments, or "giving", for political and charitable purposes. Both aspects have recently achieved greater significance, first because of proposals to amend the manner in which trade unions may impose a political levy on their members and secondly because of the philanthropic response of some companies to the tragedies of the Falklands conflict.

It should be borne in mind that companies can support political or charitable causes in ways which need not be disclosed in the annual report. They may, for example, lobby on issues on which the political parties have taken different positions, pay above normal market prices for goods or services supplied by charities, make donations in kind or second members of staff for substantial periods.

REQUIREMENTS

According to the Companies Act 1967, S.19, as updated by statutory instrument (The Companies (Directors' Report) (Political and Charitable Contributions) Regulations 1980 (S.I. 1980 No. 1055)), if, when taken together, payments for political and charitable purposes exceed £200 in total, both individual totals should be disclosed in the directors' report.

'Political purposes' refers not only to contributions to political parties themselves, but also to quasi-political bodies which may be expected to affect, directly or indirectly, the finance or public support of a political party in the UK. 'Charitable purposes' covers only payments which are exclusively charitable and therefore excludes both sponsorship, where a fairly direct commercial interest is involved, and payments to charitable bodies for services rendered.

As well as the totals referred to above, the directors' report must also reveal the recipients of political payments totalling more than £200 during the year and also specify the sum given. There is no equivalent provision relating to charitable payments.

ANALYSIS

Ease of locating information

Since a company with a particularly low level of giving does not have to make any disclosure, it is preferable that any necessary reference by other companies is made clearly, otherwise a reader might miss the data and conclude that the company's contributions were minimal and did not necessitate disclosure. As shown in Table 1, nineteen of the companies surveyed made no disclosure at all, while the majority of the remainder used a clear and unambiguous heading mentioning donations or contributions, either within the directors' report or in an appendix thereto. In eighteen cases the figures for contributions were considerably harder to find, either bearing no title or being subsumed within a more general section.

Table 1 **Ease of locating donations information**

	Large listed	Medium listed	Large unlisted	Total
Number of companies	*100*	*150*	*49*	*299*
	%	%	%	%
Specific heading	87	93	73	88
Vague heading	8	2	—	4
No heading	1	2	6	2
No disclosure.............	4	3	21	6
	100	100	100	100

Notes:
1. One private company failed to provide a copy of the directors' report and so does not enter the analysis.
2. The differences shown in this table, between the practices of the three categories of company, are statistically significant.

Compliance and content

The need to disclose the totals for both political and charitable contributions if, when taken together, they exceed £200, has been subject to differing interpretations in the literature and in practice. In the survey, 54 companies disclosed the charitable total without specifying the amount given for political purposes, which they should have done. The extent of their political contributions, if any, is therefore not clear. Table 2 summarises the disclosure of political donations.

Table 2 **The disclosure of political contributions**

	Large listed	Medium listed	Large unlisted	Total
Number of companies	*100*	*150*	*49*	*299*
	%	%	%	%
Donations acknowledged	48	35	24	38
Nil donations reported	36	44	24	38
Political data omitted	12	18	31	18
No donations disclosure	4	3	21	6
	100	100	100	100

Note: The differences shown in this table, between the practices of the three categories of company, are statistically significant.

Table 3 provides a similar survey of the disclosure of charitable contributions.

Table 3   The disclosure of charitable contributions

	Large listed	Medium listed	Large unlisted	Total
Number of companies	*100*	*150*	*49*	*299*
	%	%	%	%
Donations acknowledged	96	95	77	93
Nil donations reported	—	1	2	1
Charitable data omitted	—	1	—	0
No donations disclosure	4	3	21	6
	100	100	100	100

Notes:
1. The two companies reporting nil charitable donations also made no political contributions and therefore were not strictly required to make any disclosure.
2. The differences shown in this table, between the practices of the three categories of
   company, are statistically significant.

The details given in directors' reports enable the pattern of political giving to
be analysed. The numbers of companies supporting political parties and quasi-
political bodies are shown in Table 4, while Table 5 shows the amount of funds
involved.

Table 4   Companies supporting 'political' bodies

	Large listed	Medium listed	Large unlisted	Total
Number of companies	*48*	*52*	*12*	*112*
Donee	%	%	%	%
Conservative Party/Associations	52	63	75	60
British United Industrialists	23	19	8	20
Regional Industrialists' councils and pro-tection associations	4	13	17	10
Economic League	17	21	25	20
Centre for Policy Studies	19	8	—	12
City and Industrial Liaison Council	4	2	—	3
National Committee for Electoral Reform	4	2	—	3
Aims of Industry	10	8	—	8
Other/Unspecified	10	6	—	7

Note: Many companies support more than one donee.

Table 5 **Distribution of funds to 'political' bodies**

	Large listed	Medium listed	Large unlisted	Total
Total donations (£000)	*723*	*328*	*76*	*1127*
Donee	%	%	%	%
Conservative Party/Associations	63	65	28	61
British United Industrialists	26	15	10	22
Regional Industrialists' councils and protection associations.................	1	11	59	8
Economic League....................	4	3	3	4
Centre for Policy Studies	1	2	—	1
City and Industrial Liaison Council	1	1	—	1
National Committee for Electoral Reform	1	1	—	1
Aims of Industry.....................	1	1	—	1
Other/Unspecified	2	1	—	1
	100	100	100	100

It is sometimes difficult to determine whether a payment to an organisation falls within the definition of 'political' contained in the Companies Act 1967 S.19(3)(b). Indeed, a number of companies made their statements in terms which suggested that they were not sure whether a contribution to a certain organisation constituted a payment for political purposes. For example, Aims of Industry (once), the City and Industrial Liaison Council (twice), the Centre for Policy Studies (once), the Economic League (twice) and British United Industrialists (twice) were mentioned in terms which suggested that their inclusion was subject to some doubt. Furthermore, after stating their total for charitable giving, four companies went on to indicate that the political donations revealed represented only a sub-set of the contributions not included in the total for charitable contributions. This provides evidence for the view that some payments to quasi-political bodies are being disclosed by some companies, while similar contributions are not being revealed by other companies.

Voluntary additional disclosure

As well as that which has to be disclosed, a number of companies provided extra information. The additional disclosure can help clarify, or extend the usefulness of, the bare contributions totals and minimal detail required by statute.

For example, three companies outlined the objectives of British United Industrialists as being the furtherance of private enterprise; one of these also indicated the connection between the industrial council it supported and the Conservative Party. Generally, however, most additional disclosure was made regarding charitable contributions.

Although the previous year's figures need not be given, 75 companies provided comparative data on charitable giving. Of these, 31 also stated the previous year's political donations.

The division across company types is shown in Table 6.

Table 6   **The provision of comparative data**

	Large listed	Medium listed	Large unlisted	Total
Number of companies	100	150	49	299
	%	%	%	%
For charitable and political contributions	10	11	8	10
For charitable contributions only	10	21	6	15
No comparative figures	80	68	86	75
	100	100	100	100

Notes:
1. Of the companies providing comparative data for both political and charitable contributions, nine (= 3 + 5 + 1) made no political donations in both years. A further
   four (= 3 + 1 + 0) companies, only one (= 1 + 0 + 0) of which gave comparative
   data, stated that it was their policy not to make payments for political purposes.
2. The differences shown in this table, between the practices of the three categories of
   company, are statistically significant.

Supplementary comments on charitable donations were many and varied, but
had a tendency not to be quantified. Basically they can be divided into two
categories; those describing the financial organisation of company giving insofar
as it enables fiscal concessions to be taken advantage of, and those indicating
policy and practice regarding the distribution of donations to charitable causes.

Some companies, particularly those which have relatively large donations
programmes, use a company trust to distribute funds. Four companies
mentioned the existence of trusts, though one of these trusts had never relied on
company funds. The other three all disclosed the amount given to their trust
during the year.

Many companies make some of their charitable donations under deed of
covenant, the tax advantages of which mean that the cost of giving can be
considerably reduced if the company undertakes to make at least four equal
annual payments. Information on covenants can be useful to readers of the
annual report in assessing the extent to which the overall donations total is
flexible downwards. Six companies specifically mentioned covenants. One large
listed company gave details of a covenant, as did a medium listed company. An
unlisted company stated the destination and size of two covenants. One unlisted
and one medium listed company indicated that at least some of their donations
were made under deed of covenant, while one unlisted company revealed the
actual amount given by that method.

A number of companies which did not give any indication of the proportion of
their gifts covenanted did, however, provide at least some indication of the types
of causes they supported. Seven outlined the areas of their support, five
indicating that their giving was concentrated in reasonably specific fields; trade
charities (1), services and local charities (1), health and education (1) and
education (2). Five other companies separately disclosed the amount given for
educational purposes. Eight stated the amount they had given to the South

Atlantic Fund, established to deal with the tragedies of the Falklands conflict; another company claimed that it had made a 'substantial donation' to the Fund.

As well as the details discussed above, a number of others were voluntarily disclosed. Examples included total charitable donations made abroad and sponsorship activities. Such details can be very useful in interpreting the significance and meaning of the data required by statute which, on their own, are usually of limited use to readers of annual reports.

EXAMPLES

Two examples, which include some of the additional information discussed above, are reproduced to illustrate how it is possible to present the statutory data in a more interesting and informative way, enabling the report user to gain a clearer impression than would otherwise be the case.

Example 1
Allied-Lyons   *5 March 1983*
Directors' Report (extract):

CHARITABLE AND POLITICAL CONTRIBUTIONS
During the period companies within the group made contributions for charitable purposes totalling £169,797. This amount includes individual donations under covenant of £8,000 to Project Fullemploy, which is committed to ameliorating unemployment, and of £4,000 to the National Playing Fields Association.

It also includes donations totalling £150,000 to Allied-Lyons Charitable Trust, which was formed in February 1982 and supports a wide range of charitable causes.

Group companies sponsor a large number of community projects, sporting events and cultural activities. amongst the most well-known of these are the Arctic Lite Nations Cup darts competition and the Double Diamond Target Bowls event. Harveys of Bristol Limited have for some years sponsored concerts and recordings by the Bournemouth Symphony Orchestra and the Bournemouth Sinfonietta and the Leeds International Pianoforte Competition.

A contribution of £2,000 was made to the South Western Industrial Council (Conservative Part).

A donation of £80,000 was made to the British United Industrialists whose objectives are to further the cause of free enterprise.

Example 2
Rowntree Mackintosh   *1 January 1983*
Directors' Report (extract):

Donations
The group made charitable donations totalling £233,000 during 1982 (1981 £115,000) of which payments made by UK companies were £204,000 (1981 £83,000). These were given to a wide range of causes but many were linked to projects within the communities in which the group operates.

Two sizeable donations arose from promotional activities on confectionery brands: £64,000 to the UK children's charity "Break" which works to provide holiday and residential care for handicapped children and £50,000 to the Jimmy Savile Appeal Fund for Stoke Mandeville Hospital.

The company contributed £1,500 to Britain in Europe.

FURTHER READING

Very little has been written on political and charitable contributions in the UK, but what has been written provides useful background knowledge for understanding the reporting practices of companies. The Labour Research Department publishes regular surveys of political giving in *Labour Research* (eg, 'Tory Funds', *Labour Research* Vol. 72, No. 6 (June 1983) pp. 171–173).

Two works providing some information on the practice of company charitable giving are:

Shenfield, B., *Company Giving* (PEP Broadsheet No. 511). London: Political and Economic Planning, 1969 (out of print).
Norton, M. (ed.), *Raising Money from Industry*. London: Directory of Social Change, 1981.

Some of the information and disclosure issues are brought out in the following two preliminary articles arising from a research project funded by the Institute of Chartered Accountants in England and Wales.

Cowton, C.J., 'Company Charitable Giving: Practice and Disclosure' in *Charity Statistics 1981/82* pp. 54–56. Tonbridge: Charities Aid Foundation, 1982.
Cowton, C.J., 'Charities and Company Giving: Some Reflections' in *Charity Statistics 1982/83* pp. 16–19. Tonbridge: Charities Aid Foundation, 1983.

RESEARCH AND DEVELOPMENT

R. H. Gray

INTRODUCTION

Research and development expenditure (R & D) covers a wide range of activities whose distinguishing feature is the presence of an element of novelty or innovation. SSAP 13 "Accounting for research and development" (para 18) defines R & D as meaning expenditure falling into one or more of the following broad categories (except to the extent that it relates to locating or exploiting mineral deposits or is reimbursable by third parties either directly or under the terms of a firm contract to develop and manufacture at an agreed price which has been calculated to reimburse both elements of expenditure):

(a) Pure (or basic) research: original investigation undertaken in order to gain new scientific or technical knowledge and understanding. Basic research is not primarily directed towards any specific practical aim or application;

(b) Applied research: original investigation undertaken in order to gain new sciencific or technical knowledge and directed towards a specific practical aim or objective;

(c) Development: the use of scientific or technical knowledge in order to produce new or substantially improved materials, devices, products, processes, systems or services prior to the commencement of commercial production.

The need to account for R & D arises both from the size of the expenditure and from its importance to the future well-being of the company. R & D expenditure represents something in the region of 2% of GNP in the UK but varies considerably across industries; from less than 1% of sales, in the mechanical engineering industry to over 15% of sales in the aerospace and electronics industries, (HMSO 1980, CSO 1981). Although it is impossible to quantify accurately under the present disclosure requirements, it is clear that there are a large number of companies for whom R & D expenditures are material. Furthermore, there is evidence to suggest that R & D is strongly related with industrial success and with share price movements; that differing treatment and disclosure practices have significant economic consequences, and that the disclosure of R & D provides important information to security analysts, investors and bankers. (See Hope and Gray (forthcoming) for a review of these studies.)

There are four broad categories of problems involved in accounting for R & D.

The first is that of defining what constitutes the different categories of R & D. There are many costs such as those incurred in exploration, learning, setting up new branches or services, and marketing, for example, which are similar in nature to R & D in being expenditure incurred in the uncertain expectation of future benefit. Such costs do not, however, strictly fall within the scope of R & D as usually defined, although the dividing line is frequently hard to identify. Similarly there are difficulties in determining the point at which an activity becomes development rather than research (for example). The ASC has identified these definitional problems in each of its pronouncements and cited them as grounds for the more conservative nature of their recommendations. On the other hand, the IASC, FASB and UK Central Statistical Office have chosen to attack the problem, rather than allow it to dominate. Thus the FASB, for example, provide extensive guidance on precisely what does, and does not, constitute R & D. (FASB 1974, pp 1–6).

The second difficulty is that of matching R & D expenditures with the appropriate attributable income. The failure to develop appropriate accounting systems has meant that few companies can do this *ex post*, and so have little evidence on which to base estimates of any projects' likely *ex ante* success. Research results in this field, however, seem remarkably consistent (see e.g. Mansfield 1969 and Mansfield and Wagner 1975). Evidence seems to point to something like 50%–75% of all R & D reaching the point of 'technical' success (i.e. can be commercially exploited) and industries, taken as a whole, can normally show rates of return on R & D in excess of 20%.

The third problem is whether or not to treat R & D as an asset. The difficulty amounts to a direct conflict between the principles of matching and prudence. All R & D expenditure is undertaken in the expectation of it yielding future financial benefit. To this extent it should be treated as an asset as suggested by the more authoritative writers on accounting theory (see e.g. Sprouse and Moonitz 1962 and Hendriksen 1982). The corollary is that, in all other situations, to write off all expenditure as incurred gives a signal to the user of the accounts that the expenditure has a zero expected net realisable value. Not only is this misleading but tends to increase the incidence of economic consequences of accounting policy (see e.g. Bierman and Dukes 1975, Horwitz and Kolodny 1981). The principal argument in favour of immediate expensing is that the future benefit of R & D expenditure cannot be accurately determined and thus on practical grounds, a prudent approach is to be preferred. Despite the balance of argument tending to favour the matching principle (see e.g. Bierman and Dukes 1975, Hope and Gray, forthcoming), the ASC, IASC, and the FASB have all chosen to a greater or lesser extent, to allow prudence to dominate.

The final problem is that of determining the extent of any disclosure. As with many issues of accounting treatment, much of the above difficulties could be at least partially overcome by requiring fairly extensive disclosure which would, in turn, provide users with additional useful information. In the UK, however, concern that R & D disclosure may be misleading and may provide advantage to competitors has tended to dominate discussion of the matter, with the result that UK disclosure requirements with respect to R & D are less comprehensive than elsewhere.

REQUIREMENTS

Statutory requirements

Companies Acts prior to 1981 made no mention of research and development. R & D was therefore subject to no statutory requirements, except to the extent that it was covered by the requirements of the 'true and fair' view and those of the 1984 8th Schedule to disclose material assets. The 1981 Companies Act effectively incorporates, and thereby establishes, SSAP 13 "Accounting for research, and development", (see below). The Act prohibits pure and applied research expenditure from being treated as an asset and allows only development expenditure to be carried forward. The capitalisation of development expenditure may only take place under 'special circumstances' (undefined), and any resulting asset must be treated as a realised loss for the purposes of calculating distributable profit unless there are 'special circumstances' (undefined) justifying the directors' decision not to treat a development expenditure as a realised loss. In this latter case the reasons for the directors' decision must be disclosed in a note to the accounts. All capitalised development, however treated, carries with it the requirement to disclose, in a note to the accounts, the reasons for capitalisation and the period over which its (mandatory) amortisation is to take place (see Table 3 "Accounting policies"). There is *no* requirement to disclose the amount of either research or development expenditure (see Table 5 "Disclosure of R & D written off"). Finally the Act requires that the directors' report shall include an "indication of the activities of the company and its subsidiaries in the field of research and development" (see Table 4 "Details of R & D activities"). These requirements of the Act do not yet apply to the companies in this year's survey.

It makes an interesting contrast to note that the EEC Fourth Directive requires that *research and* development *costs* be disclosed separately, the preference being that they be treated as assets. No confident statement can be made as to why the 1981 Act failed to implement this requirement.

Standard accounting practice

Research and development is governed by SSAP 13 which became effective for accounting periods starting on or after 1st January 1978. SSAP 13 requires that all pure and applied expenditure be written off in the year in which it is incurred. Development expenditure will normally be similarly treated but paragraph 21 of SSAP 13 allows that such expenditure *may* be carried forward in the following circumstances:

(a) there is a clearly defined project, and
(b) the related expenditure is separably identifiable, and
(c) the outcome of such a project has been assessed with reasonable certainty as to
   (i)   its technical feasibility, and
   (ii) its ultimate commercial viability considered in the light of factors such as likely market conditions (including competing products), public opinion, consumer and environmental legislation, and
(d) if further development costs are to be incurred on the same project the aggregate of such costs together with related production, selling and administration costs are reasonably expected to be more than covered by related future revenues, and
(e) adequate resources exist, or are reasonably expected to be available, to enable the project to be completed and to provide any consequential increases in working capital.

Where such expenditure is capitalised, it should be systematically amortised in a way that matches the periodic costs with expected benefits. Fixed assets providing facilities for R & D should be treated in the normal way.

SSAP 13 was preceded by two exposure drafts; ED 14 which required all R & D to be immediately expensed, and ED 17 which only differed from the treatment of SSAP 13 by stating that development expenditure *should*, rather than may, be capitalised.

The disclosure requirements of SSAP 13 are minimal and apply only to deferred development expenditure. The standard requires (a) that deferred expenditure be separately disclosed and should not be included in current assets, and, (b) that opening and closing balances on the deferred development expenditure account, together with any other movements on this account be disclosed (see Table 3 "Accounting policies"). The standard also requires a statement of accounting policy, (see Table 1 "Involvement in R & D activity"). The preceding exposure drafts both required more extensive disclosure.

International accounting standards

IAS 9 "Accounting for Research and Development Activities", was issued by the IASC in July 1978. It is virtually the same as SSAP 13 except that in addition it requires disclosure of total R & D costs which are charged to expense in the period. FAS 2 "Accounting for Research and Development Costs", issued by the FASB in October 1974 is substantially similar to ED 14, in that it requires the immediate write off of all R & D costs, and requires that this figure be disclosed. Both IAS 9 and FAS 2, therefore, place much greater emphasis on disclosure than does SSAP 13. In fact, the ASC (and now the 1981 Act) are virtually alone in playing down the importance of disclosure. Not only do the IASC and the FASB consider disclosure essential but they are supported by the findings of research, by the EEC Fourth Directive and by the DoT in "The Future of Company Reports" in 1977, and by The House of Lords Select Committee in 1983. On the issue of accounting treatment however, the ASC, IASC, and FASB are in virtual agreement. That is, all three bodies have chosen to allow the principal of prudence to dominate that of accrual. Such a policy is not supported by the arguments and evidence of the literature, (see e.g. Hope and Gray, forthcoming).

General

The analysis has concentrated specifically on those companies who undertake activities that appear clearly to fall within the definition of R & D. This is different from last year when such things as 'exploration costs' were included. In cases where it was not clear whether or not the costs referred to were R & D they have been omitted. The figures therefore err on the conservative side. Despite this, and the radical change in the constitution of the survey, the total numbers are remarkably similar.

Table 1   **Involvement in R & D activity**

| | 1982–83 | | | | 1981–82 |
	Large listed	Medium listed	Large unlisted	Total	Total
Number of companies	*100*	*150*	*50*	*300*	*300*
	%	%	%	%	%
Accounting policy on R & D stated	58	44	20	45	52
Involvement with R & D specifically stated somewhere in the accounts but no accounting policy given	15	12	—	11	—
	73	56	20	56	52
Definitional problems make it difficult to determine	—	1	2	1	—
Involvement with R & D not specifically stated anywhere in the accounts but involvement probable	11	13	6	11	18
	84	70	28	68	70
Unlikely to have R & D	16	29	72	31	30
Stated as having no R & D	—	1	—	1	—
	100	100	100	100	100

Note: The differences shown in this table, between the disclosure practices of the three categories of company, are not statistically significant. The differences, between the incidence of R & D for the three categories of company, are statistically significant.

The total number of companies undertaking some R & D activity was 167 (1982–156). Of these 33 (11%) did not give an accounting policy. None of these 33 received an audit qualification. An additional 37 (12%) appeared likely to have R & D (1982–55) but made no mention of it anywhere in the annual report. These latter figures were arrived at by reference to the type of company, their industrial classification, their products and market share. The large unlisted companies generally gave significantly less information (e.g. in terms of a detailed operational review), and so their figures may be a little low. One company took the excellent step of declaring in the notes to the accounts that they had no R & D. This is a practice it would be good to see more widely adopted. There is a high proportion of the large listed companies which undertake R & D while there is a much lower proportion of the large unlisted companies which do so.

Table 2 shows the level of involvement with R & D within industrial sector. For example, 92% of medium listed engineering companies (23% out of 25%) undertake R & D, while only 6% of all retail, wholesale and distribution companies (1% out of 16%) are so involved.

Table 2   **Incidence of R & D activity by industry sector**

	1982–83				1981–82
	Large listed	*Medium listed*	*Large unlisted*	*Total*	*Total*
Number of companies ...	73 (100)	84 (150)	10 (50)	167 (300)	156
	%	%	%	%	%
Engineering (General, Electric, Chemical) ...	21 (21)	23 (25)	12 (12)	21 (21)	18
General Manufacturing ..	9 (10)	14 (18)	— (6)	10 (13)	10
Food and drink process and manufacturing	11 (17)	1 (2)	4 (6)	5 (8)	4
Retail, wholesale and distribution............	2 (13)	— (18)	— (18)	1 (16)	3
Building and civil engineering...............	3 (4)	4 (9)	— (26)	3 (11)	1
Pharmaceuticals	2 (2)	1 (1)	2 (2)	1 (1)	—
Electronics	3 (3)	2 (2)	— (—)	2 (2)	—
Aerospace	1 (1)	1 (2)	— (—)	1 (2)	—
Mining and exploration ..	2 (3)	— (2)	— (2)	1 (2)	—
Agriculture and produce	— (1)	— (1)	— (2)	— (1)	—
General group (no dominant activity)	16 (18)	7 (8)	2 (2)	9 (10)	—
Other	3 (7)	3 (13)	— (24)	2 (13)	16
	73 (100)	56 (100)	20 (100)	56 (100)	52

Note: The figures in brackets are the percentage of companies in the survey in that classification whether or not they have R & D. The large size of the 'general' classification is not particularly helpful but there was insufficient information in all but one of these cases to ascribe the R & D to a particular segment of the group's business.

Accounting policy

All the companies in the survey who undertook R & D expenditure wrote off some or all of that expenditure in the year in which it was incurred. The number of companies (1974 – 43, 1978 – 37), carrying forward development expenditure has declined markedly over the last few years of the survey. No simple explanation for this is apparent.

Table 3   **Accounting policies disclosed**

	1982–83				1981–82
	Large listed	Medium listed	Large unlisted	Total	Total
Number of companies	58	66	10	134	156
	%	%	%	%	%
All R & D revenue expense written off in the year	88	92	100	92	97
Some development expenditure carried forward recoverable under contract	5	5	—	4	3
Some development carried forward per SSAP 13	7	3	—	4	—
	100	100	100	100	100
Specifically stating a policy for R & D fixed assets.........	24	14	10	18	16
Percentage stating amortisation policy for development expenditure................	2	—	—	1	—

Note: The differences shown in this table, between the policies of the three categories of company, are not statistically significant.

Of the 6 companies carrying forward expenditure not recoverable under contract, only 1 disclosed the amount as required by SSAP 13. The remaining 5 companies did not receive audit qualifications. SSAP 13 states that R & D recoverable under contract is excepted from the standard. One of the companies in this latter category chose to give both the amount and the movement on the deferred account. Only 1 company anticipated the 1981 Act insofar as it requires the disclosure of the period over which development expenditure is amortised. This period was 5 years. The remaining 10 companies carrying forward some expenditure stated that they were reporting under the transitional section of the Act.

Disclosure

26 companies (9% of the total, 16% of those with some R & D) anticipated the 1981 Act requirement for the directors' report to include an outline of the company's R & D activities.

Table 4   **Disclosure of details of R & D activities**

	1982–83			
	Large listed	*Medium listed*	*Large unlisted*	*Total*
Number of companies	*73*	*84*	*10*	*167*
Directors report				
– extensive	11	7	10	9
– outline only	5	4	40	7
	16	11	50	16
Chairman's statement				
– extensive	5	8	—	7
– outline only	4	21	—	13
Operational review				
– extensive	19	19	30	20
– outline only	15	15	—	14
	60	75	80	69
No details given	40	25	20	31
	100	100	100	100

Note: The differences shown in this table, between the disclosure of details (outline or extensive) for the three categories of company, are statistically significant.

The distinction drawn above between 'extensive' and 'outline' is necessarily somewhat arbitrary. Where the report simply stated that certain specified branches of a group were continually seeking new products of a roughly specified type, (for example), this was treated as outline. Where companies gave a detailed description of products and methods, this was treated as extensive. Example 5 included at the end of this section represents a precise but "only just extensive" instance.

There were 4 medium listed companies who, while they specifically stated that the report and accounts complied with the reporting requirements of the 1981 Act, did not comply with this requirement to give an outline of their R & D activities. They did not receive audit qualifications.

26 companies (1982–27) chose to go beyond the minimal UK disclosure requirements and show the amount of R & D written off in the year. All but one of these gave the figure for the previous year.

Table 5 **Disclosure of R & D written off**

	1982–83 Large listed	Medium listed	Large unlisted	Total	1981–82 Total
Number of companies	73	84	10	167	156
	%	%	%	%	%
On the face of the profit and loss account..............	—	1	—	1	⎫
In the notes to the accounts ...	12	2	10	7	⎬ 14
In the directors' report	8	1	10	5	⎭
In the chairman's statement ...	2	1	—	1	3
In the operational review	4	—	—	2	—
Total disclosing expensed R & D..................	26	6	20	16	17
Depreciation on fixed assets used for R & D separately disclosed	1	—	10	1	—
Expenditure on fixed assets disclosed...................	1	—	—	1	—

Note: The differences shown in this table, between the disclosures of the three categories of company, are statistically significant.

Of the two companies which disclosed the amount carried forward, only one did this in the accounts (in current assets). This company did not show the amount written off. Only 4 companies distinguished between research or development expenditure.

Both the relative and absolute amounts spent on R & D vary considerably.

Table 6 **Size of R & D expenditure**

	1982–83 Large listed %	Medium listed %	Large unlisted %
As a percentage of capital employed			
– highest	11	9	15
– lowest	0·3	0·3	11
As a percentage of turnover			
– highest	6	6	11
– lowest	0·1	0·2	2
As a percentage of pre-tax profit/(loss)			
– highest	(138)	73	120
– lowest	1·5	2	62

continued overleaf

Average expenditure in year per disclosing company, other than on fixed assets	£68·19m	£4·4m	£33·6m

Of those not disclosing the amount:–

Number whose R & D is likely to be material	21	36	5
Number for whom it is not possible to judge	33	43	5

Some flavour of the range of commitment to R & D can be gauged from the table. For the majority of companies that did disclose R & D it represented a significant annual commitment of resources. It seemed probable that it would also be material in cases where the amount was not disclosed. The assessment of likely materiality in Table 6 has been made both by reference to the emphasis given in the annual report and by reference to the industry in which the company operated. Judging by the statements of the chairman and/or the directors, there seemed to be little doubt that R & D was considered to be an essential element of their respective businesses. It seems reasonable to presume therefore that disclosure of R & D costs might be very useful to the users of accounts.

Table 7 summarises the cases of apparent failure to comply with professional and statutory requirements. In no cases were explanations provided either in the accounts or the auditors' report. It is worth noting that the "statement by the Accounting Standards Committee on the publication of SSAP 13" specifically states that if companies choose not to comply with IAS 9, "it will be a matter which will have to be disclosed in notes to the accounts or in the auditors' report as a departure from the provisions of an international standard".

Table 7　　　　**Apparent failures to comply with requirements**

	1982-83				1981–82
	Large listed	Medium listed	Large unlisted	Total	Total
No accounting policy stated – (estimated) – SSAP 2 & 13 ..	15	18	—	33	55
Failure to disclose deferred R & D expenditure – SSAP 13	3	2	—	5	—
Failure to show movements on the deferred expenditure accounts – SSAP 13	4	2	—	6	—
Failure to disclose total R & D expenditure – IAS 9	54	79	8	141	129
Failure to supply details of R & D activities – 1981 Act..	—	4	—	4	n/a

Note: The differences shown in this table, between the three categories of company, are not statistically significant.

EXAMPLES

The first example is one of the more informative statements of accounting policy. Example 2 covers the common situation of R & D carried forward under contract. Example 3 is of a rarer type where the option to defer expenditure is taken, it is also an example of how unhelpful a policy can be when it is unsupported by disclosure. Example 4 is one of the more illuminating cases of disclosure in the accounts. Examples 5 and 6 demonstrate two approaches in the directors' report. Examples of more extensive outlines of R & D activities may be found in the accounts of Racal, Westland and Wellcome.

Example 1
The Wellcome Foundation Limited   *28 August 1982*
1. Statement of accounting policies:

(d) Research and development expenditure
Revenue expenditure on research and development is charged against profits in the year in which it is incurred. Capital expenditure on laboratories and equipment is included in fixed assets and depreciation thereon is included in the annual charge for research and development. Expenditure on patents and trade marks is also charged against profits in the year in which it is incurred.

	1982	1981
2. Profit before taxation:	**£m**	£m
The profit before taxation is stated after charging:		
Research and development expenditure		
– general	**61·9**	48·8
– depreciation	**4·4**	3·2

Example 2
Vickers plc and Subsidiary Companies   *31 December 1982*
Accounting Policies:

5. Research and development expenditure
Research and development expenditure, other than that which is recoverable on certain projects under contract with third parties, is charged against profit in the year in which it is incurred.

Example 3
London Brick plc and Subsidiary Companies   *31 December 1982*
Accounting Policies:

Research and Development
expenditure is written off in the period in which it is incurred, unless its relationship to the revenue of a future period can be established with reasonable certainty, whereupon such expenditure will be amortised over an appropriate period of time.

Note: There is no disclosure of any amount of R & D expenditure carried forward.

Example 4
Standard Telephones and Cables plc and its subsidiaries   *31 December 1982*
Accounting policies:

Research and development
All research and development expense is charged to income as incurred.

Note 11

Sales, cost of sales and expenses	Group	**£000**	£000
		1982	1981

Included in cost of sales and expenses are the following charges

Research and development:			
Expenditure, excluding costs reimbursed by customers		**33,547**	24,834
Contribution to ITT covering world-wide funding		**12,817**	12,961
Funding from ITT		**(8,818)**	(11,501)

Example 5
The Plessey Company plc   *2 April 1982*
Report of the directors:

Research and development
The Group maintains extensive laboratories and other facilities and devotes considerable effort to research and development aimed at achieving new products and processes. The Group holds 763 United Kingdom and 1,347 foreign patents. The following table compares the amounts funded by customers of the Group, on research and development during the years indicated. Figures for prior years have been restated in the light of a reclassification and redefinition of expenditure.

	Group funded £000	Customer funded £000	Total £000
1981/82	**31,672**	**103,439**	**135,111**
1980/81	25,518	102,892	128,410
1979/80	19,595	89,247	108,842
1978/79	18,512	63,909	82,421
1977/78	15,539	54,394	69,933

Example 6
Hanson Trust plc   *30 September 1982*
Report of the directors:

Research and development
Product improvement is a continuous process. Research and development to support profitable change is proceeding where necessary and such expenditure is written off in the year in which it is incurred.

Accounting policies:
(h) **Research and development**
Expenditure on research and development is written off in the year in which it is incurred.

FURTHER READING

Bierman H. and R. Dukes, "Accounting for Research Development Costs", *Journal of Accountancy*, April 1975, pp 48–55

Bullock J. and F.C. de Paula, *Research and development – the key to future profitability*, ICAEW, London, 1966

Business Monitor MO 14, *Industrial R & D by Expenditure and Employment*, HMSO 1980

Central Statistical Office, *Annual Abstract of Statistics*, 1981 Edition, pp 303–307, Government Statistical Service

Financial Accounting Standards Board, *Accounting for Research and Development Costs*, Statement of Financial Accounting Standards No 2 (FASB, October 1974)

Gellein O.S. and A.S. Newman, *Accounting for Research and Development Expenditures*, AICPA, 1973

Gray R.H. and A.J.B. Hope, "Disclosure – where auditors are failing", *Accountancy*, December 1982, pp 19–20

Hendriksen E.S., *Accounting Theory*, Irwin 1982

Hope A.J.B. and R.H. Gray, "Power and Policy Making: The Development of an R & D Standard", *Journal of Business Finance and Accounting*, Winter, 1982, pp 531–58

Hope A.J.B. and R.H. Gray, "Accounting for Research and Development – A Reassessment", (forthcoming) – copies available from the author

Horwitz B. and R. Kolodny, "The FASB, the SEC and R & D", *Bell Journal of Economics*, 1981, pp 249–62

House of Lords Select Committee on Science and Technology, 2, *Engineering research and development*, Vol 1, Report. 1983

Mansfield E., "Industrial Research and Development Characteristics, Costs and Diffusion of Results", *American Economic Review*, May 1969, p 65

Mansfield E. and S. Wagner, "Organisational and Statistical Factors Associated with Probabilities of Success in Industrial R & D", *Journal of Business*, April 1975, pp 179–98

Sprouse R.T. and M. Moonitz, "A Tentative Set of Broad Accounting Principles for Business Enterprises", *Accounting Research Study No 3*, AICPA; 1962

SEGMENTAL DISCLOSURE

C. R. Emmanuel

INTRODUCTION

Why do companies diversify? There are probably as many reasons as there are forms and degrees of diversification. Activities subject to cyclical variations are complemented with operations that maintain stable turnover and profit patterns; to high risk markets are added lower risk, lower return markets in distinct geographical locations; products with high growth potential complement those that have reached maturity. There are many dimensions by which diversification may be gauged, but perhaps the most accurate reflection is given by data that distinguish the different activities and the different geographical areas of the enterprise. Segmental reporting provides the means of disclosing an enterprise's dependence on certain business activities and geographical areas in order that users may improve their judgment about the company's past performance.

During 1983, the ASC decided to suspend the long awaited exposure draft on segmental reporting. The arguments for and against the disclosure of financial information by business activity and geographical area are well known. On the one hand, there is a genuine concern that disclosure will give competitors an advantage and that disclosure will contribute to the information over-load problem. On the other, there is the view that companies' profit, growth and risk profiles will be more clearly assessed by the users of financial reports. The improved assessment of how parts of a company have performed in the past may help to appraise future prospects and risks. By gauging the company's degree of diversification, the risks to which it is open may be evaluated and investors may be capable to making more informed investment decisions.

Research to date on the potential of segmental data to improve users' predictions of consolidated sales and earnings, often known as "predictive ability" research, is relatively scarce. In the USA, several studies have suggested that predictions of total company turnover are improved when turnover by business activity is disclosed. This finding is substantiated when using UK data, but the problems of predictive model selection, the availability of industrial statistics and the identification of reportable segments render a conclusive statement that all companies should disclose, untenable. Social reasons for supporting segmental reporting such as, improving employee relations, more open communication with consumers and host governments are less easily tested. Perhaps the most constructive input to the argument will come when empirical evidence is collected that identifies the users of segmental reports and the uses that are made of the data.

REQUIREMENTS

Statutory requirements

The Companies Act 1948, Schedule 8, para. 55 (2) requires that an analysis of turnover by different geographical markets is to be given where 'these differ substantially from each other'. This is an addition to the analysis of turnover and profit before tax among substantially different classes of business required under Section 17, Companies Act 1967. These matters are to be disclosed in the notes to the accounts, not as was the previous practice in the Director's report. These requirements apply to every set of accounts laid before the members in general meeting by every company. The exemptions for small and medium companies apply only to the version of the accounts that may be filed with the Registrar of Companies. Disclosure can be avoided by any company if the directors consider that segmental disclosure would be 'seriously prejudicial to the interests of the company', but the omission must be stated. Banking, shipping and insurance companies will comply with Schedule 8A of the Companies Act 1948 and hence adopt the disclosure requirements in Section 17 of the Companies Act 1967.

Para. 56, Schedule 8 of the Companies Act 1948 requires disclosure in the notes to the accounts of the average number of employees by categories. The categories are to be selected by the directors with regard to the way the company's activities are organised. The quality of disclosure, it is hoped, may be improved if companies adopt a categorisation basis consistent with the activity or geographical segments already identified.

Evaluation of changes

The changes incorporated in the Companies Act 1981 are minimal. The Stock Exchange Listing Agreement, para. 10(c), has required for many years a geographical analysis of turnover and of contribution to trading results of those operations carried out by the company (or group) outside the UK.

The requirements of the 1981 Act fall short of those adopted in North America and those advocated by international bodies. The standards adopted in the USA and Canada in the mid-70's require disclosure of net assets by geographical location and activity, and profit by geographical location. Nothing equivalent to the 'seriously prejudicial' clause is contained in these pronouncements and in fact, the way in which reportable industrial segments are to be identified is stated. The IASC's statement, IAS 14, on reporting financial information by segment also calls for the disclosure of identifiable assets employed by industrial and geographical segments as well as the basis on which inter-segment revenue is determined. These, and additional disclosure in respect of new capital investments by geographical area, have been advocated by the OECD and the UN. Taken in this context, it would seem that the segmental disclosure requirements of the Companies Act 1981 fall short of international developments outside the EEC.

ANALYSIS

Disclosure practice

In previous editions of this survey, the fact that many companies provide segmental data in excess of the UK statutory requirements has been noted. The analysis this year attempts to gauge differences in disclosure practice between large listed, medium listed and large unlisted companies.

Table 1   **Disclosure practice**

	Large listed	Medium listed	Large unlisted	total
		1982–83		
Number of companies	100	150	50	300
	%	%	%	%
Disclosure relative to Companies Act 1981 (Note 1)				
More than required	57	34	4	37
Same as required	12	12	—	10
Less than required	29	39	46	37
No disclosure.....................	2	15	50	16
	100	100	100	100

Notes:
1. The Companies Act 1981 requires that turnover and profit before tax for different classes of business and turnover by different geographical areas are disclosed.
2. The differences shown in this table, between the practices of the three categories of company, are statistically significant.

Voluntary disclosure of information in excess of the legal requirment is particularly notable in the case of the listed companies. This could reflect the Stock Exchange Listing requirement that profit contribution by geographical areas is disclosed. The items disclosed (see Table 2) tend to substantiate this view.

In 1968–9, 43% of the companies surveyed disclosed segmental data consistent with the prevailing statutory requirement (S.17, Companies Act 1967). For this year, 47% are consistent with paragraph 55, Schedule 8 of the Companies Act 1948 which contains the additional requirement relating to turnover by geographical area. Overall, the trend in practice appears to favour greater segmental disclosure and this is especially true in the case of the large listed companies where 69% meet or exceed the legal disclosure requirement.

In Table 2, the items disclosed are presented and the companies are additionally categorised into a group that meet or exceed the legal requirement in practice and a group that do not. One of the purposes of this categorisation is to show that companies which do not provide a segmental analysis of turnover by activity and geographical area and profit by activity nevertheless disclose some disaggregated data. The reasons for non-disclosure and for not meeting the legal requirement are presented in Table 4.

Items disclosed

Table 2   Items disclosed

Disclosure Practice

| | Meet/Exceed Companies Act 1981 | | | | Less than Companies Act 1981 | | | | |
	Large listed	Medium listed	Large unlisted	Total	Large listed	Medium listed	Large unlisted	Total	Total
Number of companies (Note 1)	69	69	2	140	29	58	23	110	250
	%	%	%	%	%	%	%	%	%
Turnover:									
by activity	100	100	100	100	66	47	83	59	82
geographically	100	100	100	100	59	52	17	46	76
Profit:									
by activity	100	100	100	100	48	36	65	45	76
geographically	74	71	100	73	28	34	13	28	53
Average number of employees:									
by activity	9	13	–	11	14	3	–	5	8
geographically	35	14	–	24	10	5	–	5	16
Net assets:									
by activity	23	10	–	16	3	2	–	2	10
geographically	29	12	–	20	17	–	–	5	13
Capital expenditure:									
by activity	17	3	–	10	7	2	4	4	7
geographically	16	1	–	9	7	–	–	2	6

Notes:
1. This table excludes the 50 companies that did not disclose any segmental data. Their reasons are presented in Table 4 together with the reasons given by the companies that did not meet the full legal requirement.
2. Three tests of statistical significance were conducted in terms of the items disclosed. They are discussed in the main body of the text.

The first test of statistical significance investigates the difference between companies who meet or exceed the legal requirement and those that do not for each item of segmental data in Table 2. There is a statistically significant difference in respect of the disclosure of turnover by activity, profit by activity and profit by geographical area. Companies that meet or exceed the legal requirement more frequently provide segmental analyses of profit by geographical area . Surprisingly, the disclosure of turnover by geographical area is not statistically significant. The companies categorised as not meeting the legal requirement of the Companies Act 1981 do provide segmental analyses but tend to supply only one or two of the items required.

The second test looked for differences between the items disclosed by large and medium listed and large unlisted companies when a) they are categorised as meeting or exceeding the legal requirement and b) when they do not. No significant differences are found in the former category. The large and medium listed companies do not seem to favour an activity or a geographical segmental analysis for the items disclosed. For those companies not meeting the legal requirement, one statistically significant relationship is apparent. Turnover by activity is more frequently disclosed than turnover by geographical area and this is most pronounced in the case of large unlisted companies. One plausible explanation is that the large unlisted companies are predominantly serving the UK home market.

The final test compared the total number of items disclosed by activity and geographical area for a) the companies categorised as meeting or exceeding the legal requirement and b) those that do not. A statistically significant difference between companies in the latter category is noted. Again, it is the large unlisted companies that favour segmental disclosure by activity and not by geographical area. There is no evidence of this trend for the companies that meet or exceed the legal requirement. When the total activity and geographical items disclosed by all companies are compared, the statistically significant difference remains. The large and medium listed companies are as likely to disclose items by means of a geographical analysis as by activity, but the large unlisted companies seem to prefer the activity analysis. If these unlisted companies are in fact only serving the UK home market, then there appears to be good reason for them not meeting the legal requirement. The same argument may apply to some of the large and medium listed companies who do no disclose segmental data consistent with the Companies Act 1981. A note in the relevant part of the annual report to state that turnover is primarily generated in the UK market would explain clearly why there is no geographical analysis.

In summary, there seems to be a wide range of items disclosed which is not fully explained by the size or listing characteristics of the companies in this survey. An impression of the range of items disclosed in addition to those given in Table 2 is provided by the following list:

The basis on which inter-segment revenue is determined	10 companies
Production or output data by activity or geographical area	9 companies
Quarterly or half-yearly results by activity or geographical area	9 companies
Current cost segmental results by activity or geographical area	5 companies

Clearly some companies are concerned to provide segmental disclosure that approximates, or even exceeds, the UN and OECD guidelines, but at present they form a minority.

Presentation adopted

In the Introduction, attention was drawn to the potential for segmental data to help users predict consolidated sales and earnings more accurately. The disclosure of previous years turnover and profit by segment activity or geographical area is necessary if trends are to be discovered. Table 3 gives the presentations adopted by those companies that meet or exceed the requirements of the Companies Act 1981.

Example 3
Baker Perkins Holdings PLC   31 March 1982
The company, principal subsidiaries and investments (all subsidiaries are wholly owned unless otherwise stated):

	Location	Country of incorporation	Business activities and products	Capital employed 31st March 1982 £000	1981 £000	Sales to customers Year to 31st March 1982 £000	1981 £000	Profit before interest and taxation Year to 31st March 1982 £000	1981 £000
EUROPE									
Baker Perkins Holdings PLC	Peterborough	United Kingdom	Parent company						
Baker Perkins Overseas Investments Ltd	Peterborough	United Kingdom	Investment company						
Baker Perkins AG	Paris and Zug	Switzerland	Investment company						
Baker Perkins Ltd	Peterborough, Basingstoke and Hebburn-on-Tyne	United Kingdom	Food, printing and foundry machinery						
Baker Perkins Chemical Machinery Ltd	Stoke-on-Trent	United Kingdom	Chemical machinery	39,014	41,324	83,678	74,886	3,681	404
Baker Perkins Guittard SA	Chelles	France	Chemical machinery						
Baker Perkins Srl	Milan	Italy	Chemical machinery						
Pavailler SA (84.8%)	Valence and Ham	France	Food machinery						
Pavailler Fratelli Monziani SpA (83%)	Milan	Italy	Food machinery						
Rose Forgrove Ltd	Leeds, Gainsborough, Gateshead, Saxilby and Skegness	United Kingdom	Packaging machinery, aeromarine specialities and spherical bearings						
Rose Forgrove GmbH	Cologne	West Germany	Packaging and food machinery						
Rose Forgrove Srl	Milan	Italy	Packaging and food machinery						
Rose Forgrove International Ltd	Stockholm	United Kingdom	Packaging and food machinery						
NORTH AMERICA									
Baker Perkins North America Inc	Baltimore, Maryland	USA	Investment company						
Baker Perkins Inc	Saginaw, Michigan	USA	Food and chemical machinery	15,764	10,341	40,545	27,551	3,802	2,325
Baker Perkins Printing Machinery Corporation	Barrington, Illinois	USA	Printing machinery						
Canadian Baker Perkins Ltd	Brampton, Ontario	Canada	Food machinery						
Rose Forgrove Inc	Chicago, Illinois	USA	Packaging machinery						
Werner Lehara Inc	Grand Rapids, Michigan	USA	Food machinery						
AUSTRALASIA									
Baker Perkins Pty Ltd	Melbourne, Brisbane, Perth and Sydney	Australia	Food and packaging machinery						
Baker Perkins Exports Pty Ltd (formerly Baker Perkins Aust Pty Ltd)	Melbourne	Australia	Food machinery	3,294	1,963	8,504	7,322	585	708
Baker Perkins (NZ) Ltd	Auckland and Christchurch	New Zealand	Food and packaging machinery						
OTHER									
Baker Perkins Far East AG	Hong Kong, Tokyo and Zug	Switzerland	Food and packaging machinery	1,164	1,227	5,075	6,720	29	690
Baker Perkins South Africa (Pty) Ltd	Johannesburg	South Africa	Food, packaging and laundry machinery						
				59,236	54,855	137,802	116,479	8,097	4,127
INVESTMENTS (See note .. on the accounts)									
Associate – Werner & Pfleiderer KG (27.2% and 100% of preference capital)	Stuttgart	West Germany	Food and chemical machinery	4,133	3,916			337	189
Others				106	36			—	—
				63,475	58,807			8,434	4,316

TOTAL GROUP (As shown by group financial statistics page .. and group profit and loss account page ..).

Table 3 Presentation adopted by companies which meet or exceed the Companies Act 1981

	1982–3			
Number of companies	Large listed	Medium listed	Large unlisted	Total
	69	69	2	140
	%	%	%	%
Turnover by activity:				
given for 1 year	16	9	–	12
2 years	71	84	100	78
3 or more years	13	7	–	10
	100	100	100	100
Turnover by geographical area:				
given for 1 year	15	19	–	16
2 years	75	78	100	77
3 or more years	10	3	–	7
	100	100	100	100
Profit by activity:				
given for 1 year	17	7	–	12
2 years	71	86	100	79
3 or more years	12	7	–	9
	100	100	100	100
Profit by geographical area:				
given for 1 year	7	9	–	8
2 years	61	61	100	61
3 or more years	6	1	–	4
Not given	26	29	–	27
	100	100	100	100
Matrix presentation	22	7	–	14

Note: The differences shown in this table, between the ways segmental data are presented by large or medium listed companies, are not statistically significant.

The most common presentation provides segmental data for the current year and the immediate, previous year. This applies to segmental analyses by activity and geographical area. The provision of two years comparative figures seems inadequate for users to discern any trend in the segmental data disclosed. It may be argued that even five years on say, turnover by activity will not reveal the underlying trend of which geographical markets are contributing to the changes in sales. For this to be seen, a matrix presentation giving turnover (or profit) by activity and geographical area is required. Twenty companies adopt this form of presentation and the format used by Cadbury Schweppes p.l.c. is given in the Examples section. There is no legal requirement or pronouncement governing the presentation of segment reports and again, practice varies widely.

Reasons for not meeting the legal requirements

Table 4   Reasons for not meeting Companies Act 1981

| | 1982–3 | | | |
	Large listed	Medium listed	Large unlisted	Total
Number of companies	31	81	48	160
	%	%	%	%
Transitional exemption (Note 1)	19	37	37	34
Single activity/seriously prejudicial (Note 2)	26	14	15	16
No reason given	55	49	48	50
	100	100	100	100

Notes:
1. 54 companies claimed transitional exemption under Schedule 2 of the Companies Act 1981 or stated that compliance with the Act was not yet required. There are 5 shipping, banking or insurance companies included here.
2. Only 2 companies, one of the large listed and one of the large unlisted, stated that disclosure was 'seriously prejudicial'.
3. The differences shown in this table, between the reasons given by the three categories of company, are not statistically significant.

The 'seriously prejudicial' justification for non-disclosure is stated by two companies only. Almost 9% of the companies surveyed state that, in the directors' opinion, a single class of business is being undertaken. In 1968-9, almost 3% of companies gave this as the reason for non-disclosure of segmental date. At present, it is extremely difficult to gauge whether the 54 companies claiming transitional exemption intend to provide segment reports in the future or whether they will take advantage of the 'seriously prejudicial' clause introduced by the Companies Act 1981. It is perhaps a sad reflection that 27% of the total number of companies in this survey do not give a reason for non-disclosure of segment reports.

EXAMPLES

A wide range of disclosure practice both in terms of content and presentation is evident from Table 2 'Items disclosed' and Table 3 'Presentation adopted'. The first example in this section shows the use of a matrix presentation to disclose the segmental data. The following examples represent innovations, with one including CCA segmental results by activity and the other indicating the product-market base of the geographical segments. The first two companies are in the large listed category and the last is from the medium listed.

Example 1
Cadbury Schweppes plc   *1 January 1983*
Sales, Trading Profit and Operating Assets Analysis:

£ million	Total	United Kingdom	Europe	America	Australia	Other
1982						
Sales						
Confectionery	**682·7**	**304·2**	**33·5**	**177·3**	**83·6**	**84·1**
Drinks	**564·7**	**203·2**	**123·5**	**127·8**	**88·5**	**21·7**
Tea and Foods	**273·9**	**218·6**	**32·6**	—	—	**22·7**
Health and Hygiene	**56·5**	**56·1**	**0·4**	—	—	—
	1,577·8	**782·1**	**190·0**	**305·1**	**172·1**	**128·5**
Trading profit						
Confectionery	**60·1**	**29·7**	**4·2**	**8·4**	**7·0**	**10·8**
Drinks	**34·3**	**8·2**	**7·8**	**11·2**	**5·9**	**1·2**
Tea and Foods	**8·5**	**5·9**	**(0·2)**	—	—	**2·8**
Health and Hygiene	**1·9**	**1·9**	—	—	—	—
	104·8	**45·7**	**11·8**	**19·6**	**12·9**	**14·8**
Operating assets						
Stock	**265·7**	**108·8**	**24·2**	**90·3**	**20·3**	**22·1**
Debtors	**240·0**	**127·2**	**26·1**	**39·0**	**18·6**	**29·1**
Creditors	**(294·6)**	**(141·7)**	**(47·8)**	**(48·3)**	**(32·0)**	**(24·8)**
	211·1	**94·3**	**2·5**	**81·0**	**6·9**	**26·4**
Land, buildings, plant and equipment	**441·3**	**224·8**	**69·6**	**66·6**	**49·5**	**30·8**
	652·4	**319·1**	**72·1**	**147·6**	**56·4**	**57·2**
1981						
Sales						
Confectionery	603·4	288·6	38·9	135·8	74·6	65·5
Drinks	386·4	184·2	55·1	48·0	77·4	21·7
Tea and Foods	237·2	191·8	24·4	—	—	21·0
Health and Hygiene	44·0	44·0	—	—	—	—
	1,271·0	708·6	118·4	183·8	152·0	108·2
Trading profit						
Confectionery	52·5	30·8	4·0	3·9	5·7	8·1
Drinks	23·4	10·7	1·5	4·8	5·3	1·1
Tea and Foods	10·8	8·2	(0·3)	—	—	2·9
Health and Hygiene	2·8	2·8	—	—	—	—
	89·5	52·5	5·2	8·7	11·0	12·1
Operating assets						
Stock	187·5	101·0	16·6	33·8	17·2	18·9
Debtors	192·5	110·0	21·0	22·0	16·7	22·8
Creditors	(213·8)	(128·2)	(23·7)	(21·4)	(27·2)	(13·3)
	166·2	82·8	13·9	34·4	6·7	28·4
Land, buildings, plant and equipment	323·9	180·4	32·8	38·6	45·3	26·8
	490·1	263·2	46·7	73·0	52·0	55·2
Trading profit to operating assets	%	%	%	%	%	%
1982	**16·1**	**14·3**	**16·4**	**13·3**	**22·9**	**25·9**
1981	18·3	19·9	11·1	11·9	21·2	21·9

Cadbury Schweppes plc   *1 January 1983*
People:

The average number of persons employed by the Company and its subsidiaries in the United Kingdom was 22,897 (1981 – 23,384). The aggregate gross remuneration including bonuses for those employees was £153·9 million (1981 – £137·6 million). The average number of employees of the Group was 38,148 (1981 – 36,463), employed in the following regions:

United Kingdom	22,897
Europe	4,949
America	2,953
Australia	3,038
Other	4,311
	38,148

Example 2
Reed International plc   *3 April 1983*
Notes on the Accounts:

26 Analysis of Turnover and Profit

£ million	Turnover		CCA Trading Profit		HCA Trading Profit	
Class of business	**1983**	1982	**1983**	1982	**1983**	1982
European Paper	**168**	174	**(1·3)**	(2·1)	**0·1**	0·8
Packaging	**280**	275	**8·2**	10·3	**14·5**	19·4
Reed Publishing	**326**	249	**24·0**	20·2	**28·1**	23·8
Consumer Publishing	**241**	252	**8·9**	0·3	**11·5**	7·1
Mirror Group Newspapers	**263**	254	**4·9**	(2·1)	**8·1**	2·1
Decorative Products	**101**	104	**(13·4)**	(16·8)	**(10·0)**	(12·4)
Paint and DIY Products	**170**	162	**6·6**	8·3	**9·6**	12·7
Reed Trading	**151**	142	**(0·5)**	(0·1)	**2·1**	3·7
Reed Building Products	**151**	133	**2·8**	4·1	**8·2**	9·0
North American Paper	**146**	141	**5·5**	14·8	**12·9**	21·4
Central Items	**—**	—	**(7·9)**	(7·6)	**(7·7)**	(6·0)
Total Turnover/Trading Profit	**1,997**	1,886	**37·8**	29·3	**77·4**	81·6
Inter-Company turnover	**(188)**	(187)				
Related Companies			**(0·1)**	1·6	**1·0**	2·5
Interest/Gearing			**(10·4)**	(4·3)	**(17·5)**	(12·5)
Turnover	**1,809**	1,699				
Profit on Ordinary Activities before Taxation:			**27·3**	26·6	**60·9**	71·6
Country of Origin						
UK	**1,502**	1,439	**31·4**	4·3	**55·7**	42·9
Europe	**153**	142	**(1·6)**	1·9	**3·0**	6·0
USA	**160**	129	**2·2**	2·5	**3·9**	4·4
Canada	**160**	153	**3·1**	18·5	**11·5**	25·6
Rest of World	**22**	23	**2·7**	2·1	**3·3**	2·7
Total	**1,997**	1,886	**37·8**	29·3	**77·4**	81·6

Geographical Market		
UK	**1,408**	1,345
Europe	**206**	198
USA	**223**	202
Canada	**79**	59
Rest of World	**81**	82
Total	**1,997**	1,886

Exports from the UK including Sales to Overseas Subsidiaries		
European Paper	**4**	3
Packaging	**7**	7
Reed Publishing	**31**	28
Consumer Publishing	**18**	18
Mirror Group Newspapers	**3**	3
Decorative Products	**13**	15
Paint and DIY Products	**10**	11
Reed Trading	**5**	5
Reed Building Products	**16**	19
Total	**107**	109

FURTHER READING

Collins, D. W., (1976), 'Predicting Earnings with Sub-Entity Data: Some Further Evidence', *Journal of Accounting Research*, Spring 1976.

Coopers & Lybrand (1977), *Analysed Reporting*, ICAEW, 1977.

Emmanuel, C.R. and Pick, R.H. (1980), 'The Predictive Ability of U.K. Segment Reports', *Journal of Business Finance and Accounting*, Vol. 7, No. 2, 1980.

Kinney, W.R. Jr. (1971), 'Predicting Earnings: Entity versus Sub-Entity Data', *Journal of Accounting Research*, Spring 1971.

Organisation for Economic Co-operation and Development (1976), International Investment – Guidelines for Multinational Enterprises', Department of Industry, 1976 (Cmnd 6525).

Ronen, J. and Livnat, J., (1981), 'Incentives for Segment Reporting', *Journal of Accounting Research*, Autumn 1981.

United Nations Economic and Social Council (1977), *International Standards of Accounting and Reporting for Transnational Corporations*, United Nations, 1977.

Additional references on this subject can be found in the reading list 'Segment reporting' available from the Library of the Institute of Chartered Accountants in England and Wales.

VALUE ADDED

P. D. Bougen

INTRODUCTION

It is sometimes contended that value added statements are essentially little more than the rearrangement of data generally available elsewhere in company accounts and as such offer little or no additional information to users. For example, although value added is not explicitly referred to in the Companies Act, 1981, two of the alternative layouts for the profit and loss account would involve the disclosure of (a) Net turnover; (b) Raw materials and consumables; and (c) other external charges, thereby enabling a measure of value added to be derived for any company which adopted one of these alternatives. However, even before the legislation of 1981, value added existed as an issue of interest to accountants. Burchell et al. (1981) trace, for example, the role of value added statements as a means of communicating financial information to employees during the 1940's and 1950's in Britain. After a decline in interest during the 1960's the value added statement re-emerged as a 'live' issue with the publication of the Accounting Standard Steering Committee's 1975 discussion paper, *The Corporate Report*, which argued (paragraph 6.7) that:

> "The simplest and most immediate way of putting profit into proper perspective vis-à-vis the whole enterprise as a collective effort by capital, management and employees is by presentation of value added (that is, sales income less materials and services purchased). Value added is the wealth the reporting entity has been able to create by its own and employees' efforts. This statement would show how value added has been used to pay those contributing to its creation".

The above definition encapsulates many of the alleged benefits claimed for the preparation and publication of value added statements. Primarily, it is argued that value added focuses attention on the success of the company to create wealth and contribute to national income. The basis for such a claim being firstly, that it is less susceptible than profit to alternative accounting treatments of key variables (for example, cost recognition and asset valuation) and secondly, that it reduces some of the difficulties involved in inter-firm comparisons generated by different industry/company characteristics such as wage levels and gearing ratios.

In addition, the rationale of the format of the statement with the emphasis being placed upon the company's performance as the collective result of the contributions of a number of groups, with associated details of the relative inducements offered to them for participation has too attracted attention. The use of value added statements as a means of communicating key financial information to employees has been supported on the basis that not only might it be more understandable than accounting profit, but also be more 'neutral' a measure by concentrating more on the relative size of payment to various coalition members than merely the payments to providers of capital. Gray and Maunders (1980) suggest that the credibility of such information might well be linked to the existence of such a statement in the audited published accounts distributed to shareholders. Related to this, has been the proposal (Cox, 1979; Morley, 1978)

151

that value added might well be a useful basis for structuring employee productivity and payment schemes.

As a reporting medium to external groups, value added could be seen as an additional element in the corporate package of financial information to assist in the prediction of key financial variables. Gray and Maunders see substantial potential here, particularly as a means of forecasting likely pay increases and hence their impact upon company profits. Finally, value added might well be viewed as a more 'socially aware' indicator of company performance by specifically recognising such performance as being the combined effort of labour, capital, management and the government. Not only might this strengthen the cohesiveness of the different groups but highlight the interactive effect of policy decision by any one of these groups upon the others.

REQUIREMENTS

There are, to date, no statutory or Stock Exchange requirements relating to value added statements. Neither have any statements of standard accounting practice nor exposure drafts been issued on the subject.

However, the major accounting bodies have commissioned a number of studies on value added statements (see Further Reading at the end of this section) most of which took as a starting point the suggestion of the Corporate Report (paragraph 6.9) that statements should contain, as a minimum, the following information:

(a) turnover
(b) bought in materials and services
(c) employees' wages and benefits
(d) dividends and interest payable
(e) tax payable
(f) amount retained for reinvestment.

In addition, the 1977 Department of Trade Consultative document 'The future of company reports" expressed the (then) Government's interest in value added. Although it was recommended that the publication and content of value added statements should be subject to general legislative requirements, none have resulted.

ANALYSIS

The number of companies producing value added statements has been falling over the last three years.

Table 1　　　　　**Value added statements provided**

	1982–3				1981–82	1980–81
	Large listed	Medium listed	Large unlisted	Total	Total	Total
Number of companies	100	150	50	300	300	300
	%	%	%	%	%	%
Statements provided	38	16	1	21	26	29
Statements not provided	62	84	99	79	74	71
	100	100	100	100	100	100

Note: The differences shown in this table, between the provision of value added statements by the three categories of company, are statistically significant.

The figures exclude a few companies which gave some information on value added but did not show its distribution and 2 (1981–82: 4) which showed the distribution of sales revenue rather than value added.

A number of observations can be made about the characteristics of companies who disclose value added statements.

1. The 38% disclosure proportion of the large listed companies indicates that size is a statistically significant factor affecting the disclosure of value added compared to the 13% evidenced by all other companies in the survey. This result is remarkably consistent with the findings of Gray and Maunders (1980) who obtained similar results with 1977/78 data.

2. An analysis was made of the industrial classifications of the companies disclosing value added. Although the sample sizes for each industry were not large enough to draw any statistically significant conclusions concerning industrial differences, a number of general observations can be made. Using the *Exstat* industrial classifications (which are also those classifications allocated by the Stock Exchange) 60 industries were represented by varying numbers of companies in the survey. 29 of these industries had at least one company disclosing value added statements. In addition, there were certain noticeable groupings of disclosure practice. So, for example, all 7 large listed companies in the brewery and distilling classifications disclosed value added, whereas none of the 10 companies in the motor distributor classifications disclosed. Again one must emphasise that whilst impossible to draw definitive conclusions from the available data, there appeared to be a greater propensity to disclose amongst manufacturing

153

industries (where adding value to products was perhaps a more physically identifiable phenomenon) than in the trading, service and commercial sectors.

3. In order to determine whether companies disclosed value added on an occasional or regular basis an analysis was made of the consistency of disclosure. Of the 64 companies who disclosed this year, 59 had done so in the previous year, 1 company had not and 4 were new to the sample. Of the 18 companies who had disclosed in the previous year but did not do so this year, 14 had been removed from the sample. Comparing the 1980–81 disclosures with this year, 56 of the 88 companies still disclosed value added, 15 did not, and 17 were no longer part of the sample. So although there is a decline in the number of companies disclosing value added, the changing structure of the sample should be considered. This is particularly relevant this year with the introduction of the large private category – where only 2 companies disclosed. Nevertheless, it is apparent that the majority of companies have never seen value added as a particularly attractive medium for the reporting of financial information to shareholders. One explanation could well be that companies view the costs of processing and presenting the information as exceeding any benefits which might accrue to users. Value added might be viewed as offering no additional information than already available from other measures of company performance. Support for this interpretation can be shown for example by the very high correlation coefficients (significant at the 99% significance level) between value added and profit arrived at from this year's survey data. It could well be that value added as a performance measure captures little that is not contained within the conventional profit figure.

One should also bear in mind that since no legislative requirements exist for value added then this too might have influenced the company's attitude towards disclosure. This might be particularly relevant because of the change of Government since the 1977 Green Paper and the early impetus which that provided for value added.

Finally if value added statements are seen as relevant to employees only, then Employee Reports might be a better vehicle for their publication than reports aimed primarily at shareholders.

Presentation

A considerable variety of styles of presentation again characterise the reporting of value added with companies reporting value added information to suit their own particular company characteristics and the perceived requirements of users.

The most popular format was a separate statement of value added which was provided in 60 cases (1981–82: 71). In 6 of these cases (as for 1981–82) there was an explicit reconciliation with profit. The alternative format was to integrate value added with other accounting statements. In one case (1981–82: 2) the value added statement was integrated with the profit and loss account, and in 3 cases (1981–82: 4) with funds flow statements.

In addition, further information was often provided to assist the user to interpret the value added measure. In 59 out of the 64 cases (1981–82: 70/77) comparative figures were provided of the previous year's value added, in four of which the figures were given for more than two years (as for 1981–82). Ratios relating to value added were provided in relatively few cases, but included (in 1982–83): value added/to assets employed; value added/to sales; and value added/to labour cost. A geographical analysis of value added was provided in 3 cases (as for 1981–82) and a divisional analysis in 1 case (as for 1981–82). Value added per employee was shown by region in 1 case (as for 1981–82) and in 1 case by division (as for 1981–82).

Diagrammatic representations accompanied the statements in 5 cases (1981–82: 14).

Audit

As already indicated, in some cases value added information formed part of another statement (i.e. profit and loss account and funds flow statement) and was covered by the audit report in that context. However in 5 cases (as for 1981–82) the audit report specifically referred to value added, whilst the statement was implicitly covered by reference to page numbers in another 8 cases (as for 1981–82).

In 1 case there was a note to the value added statement which indicated that the underlying data was based on the audited historical accounts.

Basis of calculation of value added

The Corporate Report (paragraph 6.10) suggested that value added be calculated by deducting bought in material and services from turnover, i.e. that it be gross of depreciation which would be treated as a distribution of value added. The central argument for such treatment of depreciation is what Gray and Maunders term an 'entity' approach,

". . . in that by identifying separately the funds available for reinvestment the impression is given that no particular group of stakeholders has a right to such funds but by that they will be deployed for the ultimate benefit of all".

However such an approach has attracted considerable criticism. Firstly, on the grounds that although management might have considerable power to allocate resources and thus determine depreciation independent of shareholder's wishes, nevertheless it is the shareholders themselves which have a right to such value added. The second argument is that a net basis would better emphasise the need to maintain the physical capital of the company. By computing value added net of depreciation then it is made clear that capital maintenance is secured before the rewards for participation are distributed. However the net basis itself has not escaped without criticism, perhaps the most critical being that since depreciation is a somewhat arbitrary concept then this could introduce too great a potential for the distortion of the measurement of value added for the period. This dilemma has yet to be reconciled (if indeed this is possible). Table 2 gives details of the treatment of depreciation in value added statements.

155

Table 2   Treatment of depreciation in value added statements

	\n1982–83\nLarge listed	Medium listed	Large unlisted	Total	1981–82\nTotal
Number of companies	38	24	2	64	77
	%	%	%	%	%
Value added calculated gross of depreciation	76	83	100	80	83
Value added calculated net of depreciation	13	4	–	9	10
Basis not specified	11	13	–	11	7
	100	100	100	100	100

Note: The differences shown in this table, between the treatments of depreciation for the three categories of company, are not statistically significant.

In addition several miscellaneous adjustments were sometimes made in the calculation of value added. Table 3 gives details of specific reference to the inclusion or exclusion of certain items.

Table 3   Treatment of miscellaneous adjustments

Inclusion of miscellaneous items:

	1982–83\nLarge listed	Medium listed	Large unlisted	Total	1981–82\nTotal
Number of companies	29	14	1	44	66
	%	%	%	%	%
Customs and/or excise duties ..	4	–	–	2	2
Sundry income etc.	79	79	100	80	68
Extraordinary items..........	17	21	–	18	30
	100	100	100	100	100

Exclusion of miscellaneous items:

	Large listed	Medium listed	Large unlisted	Total	Total
Number of companies	21	5	0	26	19
	%	%	%	%	%
Customs and/or excise duties ..	33	40	–	35	53
Extraordinary items..........	67	60	–	65	47
	100	100	100	100	100

Note: The differences shown in this table, between the treatments for the three categories of company, are not statistically significant.

156

Finally, some value added statements have attempted to incorporate some recognition of the effect of changing price levels upon the calculation of value added and thus also upon the availability of resources for distribution.

In 2 cases (as for 1981–82) value added was calculated on a current cost basis, thus attempting to charge against revenue of the period the current cost (usually net replacement cost) of the materials and services consumed. In 4 cases (as for 1981–82) a current cost value added statement was provided, which tried to further evaluate the impact of changing price levels usually by the inclusion of a monetary working capital and gearing adjustment.

In 3 cases the historic cost value added statement was supplemented by reference to a current cost reserve provision (1981–82: 4) and in 1 case by reference to a gearing and monetary working capital adjustment. One chose to allow for changing prices by restating all the historical data used in the value added statement in current purchasing power terms.

Distribution of value added

Most statements show value added as being divided between four categories of recipient: employees; capital suppliers; governments; and the entity itself. Descriptions of the measurement of the shares attributable to each of these groups are not always clear, but nevertheless variations in classification of items are apparent. For example, in this survey the effects of the recession have been dealt with in a variety of ways (see Table 4), some companies have seen redundancy payments as payments to employees, others, as a cost to the company itself, and in one case the subsidies received from the government for redundancy and short time working as a payment from the government. Although such a wide range of measurements can be said to reflect the particular views of the companies concerned, they do make inter-firm comparisons difficult for users and introduce considerable flexibility in determining the relative shares of value added, thereby complicating the assessment of the relative equity of payments. The information provided in the table below is intended to convey an impression of the range and distribution of measurements used to attribute relative shares in value added to the four categories mentioned above.

Table 4   **Measurement of relative shares of value added**

	1982–83				1981–82
	Large listed	Medium listed	Large unlisted	Total	Total
Number of companies	38	24	2	64	77
	%	%	%	%	%
Employees shown as:					
pay and pension contributions...................	26	21	50	25	30
pay, pensions and social security contributions	21	29	50	25	26
pay and related costs or benefits	18	13	–	16	12
net (of tax) pay and related costs or benefits	3	13	–	6	6
gross pay and related costs or benefits	5	8	–	6	10
pay (etc.) and profits sharing	8	4	–	6	4
pay (etc.) and redundancy payments...............	11	8	–	10	6
measurement not clear	8	4	–	6	6
	100	100	100	100	100
Capital suppliers, shown as:	%	%	%	%	%
dividends.................	3	8	–	5	4
dividends and minority interest earnings	–	–	–	–	1
interest and dividends	31	50	100	41	39
interest, dividends and minority interests	58	25	–	44	51
interest, and minority interests	–	4	–	2	1
interest	5	4	–	4	1
measurement not clear	3	9	–	4	3
	100	100	100	100	100

Number of companies	Large listed	Medium listed	Large unlisted	Total	Total
		1982-83			1981–82
	38	24	2	64	77
Government (central and local) shown as:	%	%	%	%	%
corporate taxes	71	72	–	69	77
taxes, duties and levies	3	–	–	2	1
taxes and social security contributions	–	–	–	–	1
corporate and sales taxes	–	4	–	1	1
taxes and rates	3	–	100	5	1
corporate taxes, social security contributions and PAYE	–	4	–	1	1
corporate taxes, social security, rates, PAYE etc.	–	8	–	3	3
corporate taxes, salary deductions, rates, duties, levies, sales taxes	3	–	–	2	4
corporate taxes net of grants received from central government or EEC	10	–	–	5	5
taxes net of government subsidies for redundancy and short time workers	–	4	–	2	–
measurement not clear	10	8	–	10	6
	100	100	100	100	100
Residual share shown as:	%	%	%	%	%
retained profits	21	8	–	16	16
depreciation	3	–	–	1	4
depreciation and retained profit	55	63	100	60	66
depreciation, retained profits and minority interests	5	8	–	6	6
depreciation, retained profits and deferred tax	3	8	–	5	3
retained profits and minority interests	–	4	–	1	3
retained profits and planned closure costs	5	–	–	3	1
depreciation and lease re-purchase provision	3	–	–	1	–
measurement not clear	5	9	–	7	1
	100	100	100	100	100

Notes:
1. One company (1981–82: 2) which showed Government's share as corporate taxes in the statement also showed collections on behalf of Government (i.e. PAYE, VAT and Social Security contributions) as a note.
2. The differences shown in this table, between the measurement bases for the three categories of company, are not statistically significant.

EXAMPLES

The example of Colt International has many interesting features:

(1) It is remarkable in that the value added statement is given central prominence in the accounts, with the 'Statement of the Results of the Group' in effect replacing the conventional Profit and Loss Account.

(2) The wealth of value added information contained in the accounts is exemplary.

(3) Although it is one of only two private companies in the survey which disclosed value added statements, it indicates that value added can be a feasible and useful vehicle for financial disclosure to other than the large listed company.

Example 1
Colt International   *31 December 1981*
Extract from the Report of the Directors:

4. Financial Highlights	**1981** **£000**	1980 £000
Value of Colt goods and services provided to customers (turnover)		
Environmental control	**37,259**	34,923
Precision engineering	**2,333**	2,316
	39.592	37,239
Value created by our efforts was	**17,723**	18,096
This was divided as follows		
To Colt personnel in wages, salaries, pension and employment benefits	**16,093**	15,297
In taxes and levies to local authorities	**335**	292
In interest to banks and other institutions who provide financial resources	**455**	388
Retained to provide for the replacement of our machinery and other equipment which wears out through use	**640**	620
Leaving a net value before taxes to national governments	**200**	1,499
This net value was contributed by the following activities		
Environmental control	**434**	1,537
Precision engineering	**(234)**	(38)
	200	1,499
This net value was then divided as follows		
From our partners in those Colt companies which are not wholly owned by the Colt Group	**(111)**	29
In dividends to shareholders	**29**	139
In taxes to national governments	**76**	382
Retained in the business to provide additional resources to strengthen and expand Colt activities	**206**	949
	200	1,499

Statement of the Results of the Group:

	Note	1981 £000	1981 £000	1980 £000	1980 £000
The value of Colt goods and services provided to customers during the year amounted to	.., ..		**39,592**		37,239
To supply these goods and services we purchased materials and services to the value of	..		**21,869**		19,143
The value created by our efforts was			**17,723**		18,096

This added value was divided as follows

To Colt personnel

In wages, salaries, pensions and employment benefits	..		**16,093**		15,297
In taxes and levies to					
National governments	..	**76**		382	
Local authorities		**335**	**411**	292	674
To those who provide financial resources					
Bank and loan interest	..	**455**		388	
Dividends to shareholders	..	**29**	**484**	139	527
From our partners in those Colt companies					
Which are not wholly owned by the Colt Group			**(111)**		29
Retained within the Colt Group					
To provide depreciation for the replacement of our machinery and other equipment which wears out through use	.., ..	**640**		620	
To provide additional resources to strengthen and expand Colt activities	..	**206**	**846**	949	1,569
			17,723		18,096

Net Group revenue is as shown in the Statement of Source and Application of Funds on page . ..

161

Group Financial Results 1974–1981:

Results Adjusted for Inflation

The Statement below attempts to show the effects of inflation on the business by restating the historical values shown in the accounts in relation to the purchasing power of the £ at 31st December 1981 using general indices of prices.

	Historical Values								Current Purchasing Power Values							
	1974 £000	1975 £000	1976 £000	1977 £000	1978 £000	1979 £000	1980 £000	1981 £000	1974 £000	1975 £000	1976 £000	1977 £000	1978 £000	1979 £000	1980 £000	1981 £000
The value of Colt goods and services provided to customers during the year amounted to	16,881	16,280	22,558	29,206	32,878	37,814	37,239	39,592	47,217	36,481	43,310	49,103	50,906	51,179	43,213	41,068
To supply these goods and services we purchased materials and services to the value of	8,959	7,877	10,388	14,568	16,552	18,942	19,143	21,869	25,807	18,688	20,575	25,216	26,353	26,515	23,235	23,393
The value created by our efforts was	7,922	8,403	12,170	14,638	16,326	18,872	18,096	17,723	21,410	17,793	22,735	23,887	24,553	24,664	19,978	17,675
Net monetary gain/(loss) arising from adjustments for the effects of inflation	—	—	—	—	—	—	—	—	493	650	247	378	(52)	(255)	(84)	(333)
Total Added Value	7,922	8,403	12,170	14,638	16,326	18,872	18,096	17,723	21,903	18,443	22,982	24,265	24,501	24,409	19,894	17,342
The Added Value was divided as follows:																
To Colt Personnel																
In wages, salaries, pension and employment benefits	5,654	6,729	8,850	10,984	12,758	14,661	15,297	16,093	15,847	15,133	17,057	18,490	19,786	19,869	17,774	16,723
In Taxes and Levies to																
National governments	367	730	1,069	885	992	1,482	382	76	970	1,544	1,965	1,450	1,499	1,912	428	76
Local authorities	126	141	238	244	177	248	292	335	357	324	454	412	277	341	341	351
To those who provided Financial Resources																
Bank and loan interest	201	157	57	35	186	261	388	455	564	352	105	58	292	351	448	472
Dividends and shareholders	12	13	14	37	259	270	139	29	34	29	27	62	396	348	156	29
To our Partners in those Colt companies which are not fully owned by the Colt Group	(4)	9	7	11	158	124	29	(111)	1	18	(11)	(55)	234	130	(40)	(155)
Retained within the Colt Group																
To provide depreciation for the replacement of our machinery and other equipment which wears out through use	266	288	313	391	438	620	620	640	897	840	835	903	681	933	865	754
To provide additional resources to strengthen and expand Colt activities	1,300	336	1,622	2,051	1,358	1,206	949	206	3,233	203	2,550	2,945	1,336	525	(78)	(908)
	7,922	8,403	12,170	14,638	16,326	18,872	18,096	17,723	21,903	18,443	22,982	24,265	24,501	24,409	19,894	17,342

FURTHER READING

Burchell, S., Clubb, C. and Hopwood, A., "A Message from Mars and other reminiscences from the past", *Accountancy*, October, 1981.

Burchell, S., Clubb, C. and Hopwood, A., *Accounting in its Social Context: Towards a History of Value Added in the U.K.*, Working Paper, London Business School, 1981.

Cox, B., *Value Added – an appreciation for the accountant concerned with Industry*, Institute of Cost and Management Accountants, 1979.

Gray, S. J. and Maunders, K. T., *Value Added Reporting: Uses and Measurement*, Association of Certified Accountants, 1980.

Morley, M. F., *The Value Added Statement. A review of its uses in Corporate Reports*, ICAS, 1978.

Morley, M. F., "Value Added: the fashionable choice for annual reports and incentive schemes", *The Accountant's Magaazine*, June, 1979.

Renshall, M., Allan, R. and Nicholson, K., *Added Value in External Financial Reporting*, ICAEW, 1979.

Rutherford, B. A., "Value Added as a Focus of Attention for Financial Reporting: Some Conceptual Problems", *Accounting and Business Research*, Summer, 1977.

McLeay, S., "Value Added: a comparative study", *Accounting, Organizations and Society*, Vol. 8, No. 1, 1983.

APPENDIX 1

INTRODUCTION

This appendix describes the technical characteristics of the sample of companies on which this survey is based. It also describes the use of tests of statistical significance applied to the analysis tables. Finally, it lists the companies who supplied multiple copies of their accounts from which the sample is drawn.

SAMPLE SELECTION CRITERIA

The research in this series of surveys is intended to reflect the financial reporting practices of the largest UK companies. The companies are chosen for analysis on the basis of the following general criteria:

1 they have published their annual report and accounts during the year ended 30th June 1983; and
2 they are not subsidiaries of other companies in the survey.

Starting with the current edition, the companies are divided into three categories, each of which are chosen on the basis of the following additional criteria:

Large listed companies

3 they have an equity listing on the London Stock Exchange; and
4 they are ranked in the top 200 of *The Times 1000*.

Medium listed companies

3 they have an equity listing on the London Stock Exchange; and
4 they are ranked in the range 201 to 750 of *The Times 1000*.

Large unlisted companies

3 they do not have a listing of any securities on the London Stock Exchange, but they are nevertheless companies controlled within the UK; and
4 they are ranked in the top 750 of *The Times 1000*.

STATISTICAL SIGNIFICANCE OF THE TABLES

Starting with the current edition, this survey reports on the statistical significance of the tables presented in the analysis sections. The objective is to distinguish between differences in the tables which have occurred by chance and those which reflect underlying differences between the reporting practices of the three categories of company.

In this survey, the statistical significance of the tables is tested using the chi-square statistic at the 5% level. This means that a table is only reported as being statistically significant if the differences shown have occurred by chance with a probability of 0·05 or less.

165

COMPANIES INCLUDED IN THIS SURVEY

The editors are most grateful to the following listed companies for providing multiple copies of their accounts for analysis.

A. A. H.
Aberdeen Construction Group
Acrow
Adwest Group
AE
Albright & Wilson
Allied Lyons
Amalgamated Metal Corporation
Appleyard Group Companies
APV Holdings
Armstrong Equipment
Associated Dairies
Associated Fisheries
Associated Newspapers
Aurora Holdings
Automotive Products
Avon Rubber Co.
Babcock International
Wm. Baird & Co.
Baker Perkins Holdings
Barratt Developments
Barton Group
Bass
BAT Industries
Bath and Portland Group
B.B.A. Group
Beecham Group
Bejam Group
Arthur Bell & Sons
S. & W. Berisford
Bestobell
J. Bibby & Sons
BICC
Birmid Qualcast
Bishop's Group
Blackwood Hodge
Blue Circle Industries
BOC Group
Booker McConnell
Boots Co.
Henry Boot & Sons
Thomas Borthwick & Sons
B.P.B. Industries
Bridon
British Aerospace
British Home Stores
British Petroleum Co.
British Sugar Corpn.
British Vita Co.
BPCC

Brockhouse
Brooke Bond Liebig
John Brown
Brown Boveri Kent
Bryant Holdings
BSG International
BSR
BTR
Bunzl
Burmah Oil Co
Burnett & Hallamshire Holdings
Burton Group
Cadbury Schweppes
Cape Industries
Capper-Neill
Carpets International
Central & Sheerwood
Charterhouse Group
Chloride Group
Chubb & Son
Coalite Group
Coates Bros. & Co.
Coats Patons
Wm. Collins
Combined English Stores Group
Comet Group
Conder International
Consolidated Gold Field
Cookson Group
Cope Allman International
Costain Group
Courtaulds
Croda International
Crown House
Currys
Dalgety
Danish Bacon Co.
Davies & Newman Holdings
Godfrey Davis
Davy Corp.
Dawson International
De La Rue Co.
Delta Group
Distillers Co.
Dixons Photographic
Dobson Park Industries
Dorada Holdings
Robert M. Douglas Holdings
Dowty Group
Drake & Scull Holdings

Dunlop Holdings
Duport
English China Clays
Electronic Rentals Group
B. Elliott Group
Empire Stores (Bradford)
European Ferries
J. H. Fenner & Co. (Holdings)
Ferranti
Fine Art Developments
James Finlay & Co.
Fisons
Fitch Lovell
FMC
John Folkes Hefo
Foseco Minsep
Freemans (London SW9)
French Kier Holdings
Gestetner Holdings
Gill & Duffus Group
Glaxo Holdings
Glynwed
Grampion Holdings
Granada Group
Grand Metropolitan
Grattan
Great Universal Stores
Greenall Whitley & Co.
Guest, Keen & Nettlefolds
Arthur Guinness Son & Co.
Guinness Peat Group
Habitat Mothercare
Haden
Hall Engineering (Holdings)
Mathew Hall & Co.
Hanger Investments
Hanson Trust
Hargreaves Group
Harris Queensway Group
T. C. Harrison
Harrisons & Crosfield
Hartwells Group
Hawker Siddeley Group
H. J. Heinz Co.
Henlys
Hepworth Ceramic Holdings
Heron Corporation
Hewden-Stuart Plant
Hickson & Welch (Holdings)
Higgs & Hill
Hillards
Amos Hinton & Sons
Hoover
House of Fraser
Howard Machinery
Howden Group
Hunting Associated Industries

Horizon Travel
Ibstock Johnsen
ICL
IMI
Imperial Chemical Industries
Imperial Continental Gas Assoc.
Imperial Group
Inchcape & Co.
Initial
William Jackson & Son
Johnson & Firth Brown
Johnson Matthey & Co.
Kenning Motor Group
Kwik Save Discount Group
Ladbroke Group
Laird Group
Laporte Industries (Holdings)
LCP Holdings
Lee Cooper Group
Lennons Group
John Lewis Partnership
Lex Services Group
F. J. C. Lilley
Linfood Holdings
London Brick Co.
London & Northern Group
Lonrho
Y. J. Lovell (Holdings)
Low & Bonar
Wm. Low & Co.
LRC International
Lucas Industries
Macarthys Pharmaceuticals
Donald MacPherson Group
Magnet & Southerns
Marchwiel
Marks & Spencer
Marley
Martin the Newsagent
McCorquodale & Co.
McKechnie Bros.
John Menzies (Holdings)
Metal Box
Metal Closures Group
Meyer International
MFI Furniture Group
Mitchell Cotts Group
Molins
Monsanto
Morgan Crucible Co.
Wm. Morrison Supermarkets
John Mowlem & Co.
Newarthill
News International
Norcros
Northern Engineering Industries
Northern Foods

Nottingham Manufacturing Co.
NSS Newsagents
Nurdin & Peacock
Ocean Transport & Trading
Owen & Owen
Paterson Zochonis
Pauls & Whites
S. Pearson & Son
Pegler-Hattersley
Peninsular & Oriental Steam Nav. Co.
Pentos
Harold Perry Motors
Pilkington Bros.
Pirelli General
Plessey Co.
Portals Holdings
Powell Duffryn & Co.
Pritchard Services Group
H. J. Quick Group
Racal Electronics
Rank Organisation
Readicut Int.
Reckitt & Colman
Redland
Reed International
Renold
Rentokil Group
RHP Group
Rio Tinto-Zinc Corp
RMC Group
Robertson Foods
Rockware Group
Rothmans International
Rowntree Mackintosh
Rugby Portland Cement Co.
Rush & Tompkins Group
J. Sainsbury
H. Samuel
Sangers Group
Scapa Group
Scottish & Newcastle Breweries
Sears Holdings
Securicor Group
Sedgwick Group
SGB Group
Shell Transport & Trading

Simon Engineering
600 Group
Smith & Nephew Assoc. Companies
W. H. Smith & Sons (Holdings)
Smiths Industries
Standard Telephone & Cables
Staveley Industries
Steel Bros. Holdings
Steetley Co.
Stenhouse Holdings
Tarmac
Tate & Lyle
Taylor Woodrow
Telefusion
Thorn EMI
Thomas Tilling
TI Group
Tioxide Group
Tootal
Tozer, Kemsley & Milbourn (Holdings)
Trafalgar House
Transport Development
Travis & Arnold
Tricentrol
Trident Television
Trusthouse Forte
Turner & Newall
Turriff Corporation
UBM Group
UDS Group
Unigate
Unilever
United Biscuits (Holdings)
United Glass
Vantona Group
Vickers
Ward & Goldstone
Ward White Group
Wedgewood
Weir Group
Westland Aircraft
Whitbread & Co.
Whitecroft
George Wimpey
Wolseley Hughes
F. W. Woolworth & Co.

The editors are most grateful to the following unlisted companies for providing multiple copies of their accounts for analysis.

W. S. Atkins Group
Charles Barker
Bayford
Belling & Company
Alfred Booth
British Bloodstock Agency
A. F. Budge
James Burrough
Joseph Cartwright
Chiltern Motors
Christian Salvesen
C. & J. Clark
James Clark & Eaton
Colt International
Coutinho Caro
Derek Crouch
Crystal of Hull
Davies Turner
Espley Tyas Construction
J. Evershed & Son
Geest Holdings
Charles Gray Builders
Heron International
Robert Horne
John Howard

Humphrey Brothers
Jebsen Drilling
H. A. Job
James A. Laidlaw
Lancer Boss
MacMillan
May Gurney
Napier Brown
OCS Group
Palmer & Harvey
Frederick Parker
Sandell Perkins
John Silver Holdings
Socomex
John Swire
G. Percy Trentham
Daniel Thwaites
Usbourne & Son
G. E. Wallis
Warburtons
Weetabix
Wellcome Foundation
John Willmott
John E. Wiltshier
John Wood

APPENDIX 2

CUMULATIVE CONTENTS LIST

These cumulative contents pages indicate where the latest analysis of each aspect of financial reporting can be found in this series of annual surveys. The need for cumulative contents pages arises from the change in editorial objectives, set out in the Editorial Introduction, in which some aspects of financial reporting practice will be surveyed less frequently than others.

The first line of each entry indicates the edition in which the analysis can be found.

	Page
Recent developments E. C. M. Barnes	**1983–84**
Company law	1
Companies Act 1981	1
Companies Act 1981 and SSAP 9	3
Companies (Beneficial Interests) Act 1983	3
Companies (Accounts) Regulations 1982	3
Employment Act 1982	4
EC Seventh Company Law Directive	4
UK accounting standards	4
The standard setting process	4
Public sector liaison group	5
UK Statements of Standard Accounting Practice	5
UK Exposure Drafts	5
UK Discussion Papers	7
Current cost accounting	8
Examples	9
Additional dimensions of corporate reporting P. D. Bougen	**1982–83**
Introduction	150
Analysis	152
Statement of money exchanges with government	152
Statement of transactions in foreign currency	152
Statement of future prospects	152
Statement of corporate objectives	152
Example	152
Associated companies R. A. Wyld	**1983–84**
Introduction	15
Requirements	15
Analysis	17
Associated company treatment	17
Reasons given for not using associated company treatment	18
Disclosure of attributable results of associated companies	18
Associated companies in the consolidated balance sheet	19
Definition of an associated company	19
Conclusion	20
Examples	21
Further reading	22

Auditors' report   *C. J. N. Williams* **1982–83**
   Introduction.. 27
   Requirements 27
   Analysis 30
      Qualifications in auditors' reports 31
      Emphasis of matter in the auditors' report 32
      References to accounting convention 33
      References to current cost accounts 34
      Audit of value added statements 34
      Accounts not audited by the auditors of the holding company 34
      References to other auditors 35
      Dating of auditors' report............................ 35
      Reference to auditing standards 36
   Examples 36
 Further reading 38

Contingencies and commitments
   D. M. C. E. Steen and R. M. Wilkins **1982–83**
   Introduction.. 39
   Requirements 39
   Analysis 40
      Types of contingency disclosed 41
      Commitments 42
   Examples 42
      Further reading...................................... 43

Current cost accounting   *J. H. Plowdon and D. P. Tweedie* **1983–84**
   Introduction.. 23
   Requirements 24
      Statutory requirements.............................. 24
      Standard accounting practice........................ 24
   Analysis 26
      Introduction.. 26
      The impact of current cost adjustments on historical cost profit before
        taxation.. 26
      Failure to provide current cost statements 29
      Problems of companies complying with the standard 33
      Bases adopted for assessing current cost valuations and adjustments.. 36
      General.. 39
   Example 40
   Further reading 47

Earnings per share   *D. M. C. E. Steen and R. M. Wilkins* **1982–83**
   Introduction.. 69
   Requirements 69
   Analysis 70
      Disclosure where a loss per share 70
      Disclosure of basis of calculation...................... 70
      Information on diluted earnings 71
      Disclosure of earnings on the nil distribution basis 71
      Disclosure of additional earnings per share information 72
   Examples 73

Equity investments *C. J. N. Williams* **1982–83**
  Introduction 134
  Requirements 134
    Analysis 134
    Listed investments 135
    Unlisted investments 135
  Examples 136

Extraordinary items and changes of accounting policy
  J. M. Cholmeley **1982–83**
  Introduction 74
  Requirements 74
    Statutory requirements 74
    Standard accounting practice 74
  Analysis 75
    Definition of exceptional, extraordinary and other items 76
    Disclosure of exceptional items 78
  Examples 79

Fixed assets *J. P. Carty* **1983–84**
  Introduction 49
  Requirements 49
    Statutory requirements 49
    Standard accounting practice 50
    International standards 50
  Analysis 51
    Presentation 51
    Classification of fixed assets 51
    Valuation of fixed assets in HCA 52
    Government grants 54
    Directors' statements on the market value of property 54
    Investment property 56
    Valuation of fixed assets in CCA 57
    Depreciation 58
    Asset lives for current costing accounts 61
  Examples 62
  Further reading 63

Foreign currencies *S. J. Gray and C. B. Roberts* **1983–84**
  Introduction 65
  Requirements 66
    Statutory requirements 66
    Standard accounting practice 67
    International accounting standards 68
  Analysis 68
    Accounting policies 68
    Translation methods 69
    Treatment of exchange differences 70
    Impact of exchange differences 76
    Disclosure of additional information 78
    Summary and conclusions 81

Examples 81
Further reading 85

Group Accounts   *D. M. C. E. Steen and R. M. Wilkins* **1983–84**
Introduction 87
Requirements 87
   Form of group accounts 87
   Accounting dates 88
   Minority interests 88
   Changes in the composition of a group 89
   Treatment of goodwill 90
   Holding company accounts 91
Analysis 92
   Exclusion from consolidation 92
   Accounting dates 93
   Minority interests 95
   Changes in the composition of a group 96
   Treatment of goodwill 99
   Investments and other interests in subsidiaries in the accounts of
      holding companies 101
Examples 103
Further reading 106

Historical summaries   *W. D. R. Swanney* **1982–83**
Introduction 137
Requirements 137
Analysis 137
   Periods covered by historical summaries 138
   Information provided in historical summaries 138
   Reference to the effect of inflation 139
Examples 140
Further reading 142

Interim reports   *J. M. Cholmeley* **1982–83**
Introduction 113
Requirements 113
   Stock Exchange requirements 113
Analysis 114
   Form and timing of publication 114
   Historical cost profit and loss information 115
   Current cost profit and loss information 116
   Dividend distributions 117
   Balance sheet and other accounting information 117
   Trading conditions and forecasts 117
Examples 119
Further reading 121

Leasing and hire purchase   *R. Brandt and P. F. Green* **1982–83**
Introduction 122
Requirements 123
   Statutory requirements 123
   Standard accounting practice 124
   International accounting standards 125

Analysis 125
   Asset disclosure by lessors 127
   Income disclosure by lessors 128
   Income recognition policies of lessors........................ 128
   Depreciation policies of lessors 129
   Finance leases, hire purchase and instalment credit agreements of
     lessees 130
   Operating leases, hire purchase and unidentified leases of lessees 131
Examples 131
Further reading 133

Pension costs   *C. J. Napier* **1983–84**
Introduction 107
Requirements 108
   Statutory requirements....................................... 108
   Standard accounting practice 108
   International standards....................................... 109
Analysis 110
   Number of items disclosed 110
   Pension expense 112
   Actuarial involvement 112
   Miscellaneous disclosures.................................... 114
Examples 115
Further reading 116

Political and charitable contributions   *C. J. Cowton* **1983–84**
Introduction 117
Requirements 117
Analysis 117
   Ease of locating information 118
   Compliance and content...................................... 118
   Voluntary additional disclosure 120
Examples 122
Further reading 123

Post balance sheet events   *W. D. R. Swanney*...................... **1982–83**
Introduction 143
Requirements 143
   Statutory requirements....................................... 143
   Standard accounting practice 143
Analysis 143
   Types of post balance sheet event referred to in annual reports 144
Examples 144
Further reading 145

Research and Development   *R. H. Gray* **1983–84**
Introduction 125
Requirements 126
   Statutory requirements....................................... 126
   Standard accounting practice 127
   International accounting standards 128

Analysis   129
   Involvement in R & D Activity   129
   Incidence of R & D by industry sector   130
   Accounting policies disclosed   131
   Method of disclosure of details of R & D activities   132
   Disclosure of R & D written off   133
   Size of R & D expenditure   133
   Apparent failure to comply with requirements   134
Examples   135
Further reading   137

Reserves   *W. D. R. Swanney* **1982–83**
Introduction   146
Requirements   146
   Statutory requirements   146
   Standard accounting practice   146
Analysis   147
   Classification of reserves   147
Examples   148

Segmental disclosure   *C. R. Emmanuel* **1983–84**
Introduction   139
Requirements   139
   Statutory requirements   139
   Evaluation of changes   140
Anaylsis   140
   Disclosure practice   140
   Presentation adopted   143
   Reasons given for not meeting the legal requirements   146
Examples   146
Further reading   149

Simplified and employee reports   *K. T. Maunders* **1982–83**
Introduction   173
Requirements   173
Analysis   174
   Highlights of the year statements   174
   Production of simplified reports   175
   Distribution of reports   175
   Principal contents of simplified reports   176
Examples   176
Further reading   177

Social reporting and the employment report   *K. T. Maunders* **1982–83**
Introduction   178
Requirements   180
   Statutory requirements   180
   Standard accounting practice and Stock Exchange requirements   181
Analysis   181
   Categories of information in social reports   181
   Disclosure of employment information in excess of Companies Act
      requirements   182

    Health and safety statement 182
    Policy on disabled persons 183
    Other information 183
  Examples 183
  Further reading 187

Sources and applications of funds   *J. P. Carty* **1982–83**
  Introduction 188
  Requirements 188
    Standard accounting practice 188
  Analysis 189
    Period covered 190
    Status of the statement 190
    Impact of funds statement 190
    Current cost accounting 190
    Format 191
    Net liquid funds and working capital 191
    Profit or loss in the funds statement 193
    Extraordinary items 193
    Minority interests 194
    Associated companies 194
    Taxation 195
    Dividends 195
    Depreciation and capital investment 196
    Investing activities 196
    Foreign exchange differences 196
    Conclusions 197
  Examples 198
  Further reading 200

Stocks and work in progress   *D. M. C. E. Steen and R. M. Wilkins* . . . **1982–83**
  Introduction 201
  Requirements 201
    Statutory requirements 201
    Standard accounting practice 201
  Analysis 202
    Categories of stocks 202
    Bases of calculation 203
    Disclosure of methods used to calculate cost 204
    Disclosure of treatment of overheads 205
    Treatment of work in progress on long term contracts 206
  Examples 207
  Further reading 208

Taxation   *R. Brandt and P. F. Green* **1982–83**
  Introduction 209
  Requirements 209
    Statutory requirements 209
    Standard accounting practice 210
    Other requirements 212

Analysis 212
   Disclosure of corporation tax liabilities 213
   Advance corporation tax:
      Profit and loss account treatment 214
      Disclosure of irrecoverable ACT 214
   Franked investment income 215
   Overseas taxation 216
   Deferred taxation:
      Accounting policies 216
      Profit and loss account presentation 218
      Balance sheet presentation 219
      Accounting for stock relief 220
      Disclosure of full potential tax liability 221
      Scope and extent 221
   Special circumstances affecting the tax charge 222
   Close companies 223
   Examples 224

Value added *P. D. Bougen* **1983–84**
   Introduction 151
   Requirements 152
   Analysis 153
      Value added statements provided 153
      Presentation 154
      Audit 155
      Basis of calculation of value added 155
      Distribution of value added 157
   Examples 160
   Further reading 163

Pension funds *W. D. R. Swanney* **1982–83**
   Introduction 236
   Requirements 236
      Statutory requirements 236
      Standard accounting practice 237
      Other guidelines and recommendations 238
   Analysis 238
      General format of reports 238
      Information included in trustees' reports 239
   Investment statistics 239
   Statement of accounts 240
      Accounting policies 240
      Contents of accounts and notes 242
      Auditor's reports 242
      Frequency of actuarial valuations 244
      Information on actuarial valuations included in annual reports 244
   Examples 245
   Further reading 247
   Pension funds included in the survey 247

Property companies   *W. D. R. Swanney* **1982–83**

    Introduction 248

    Requirements 248

        Statutory requirements 248

        Standard accounting practice 249

        Other disclosures 249

    Analysis 250

        Presentation of properties in the balance sheet 250

        Surpluses and deficits on revaluations and sales 251

        Presentation of reserves and results for the year 251

        Identification and treatment of development costs 251

        Contingent tax liability on revaluation surplus 252

        Depreciation of properties 252

    Examples 253

    Further reading 255

    Property companies included in the survey 255

Appendix **1983–84**

    Introduction 165

    Sample selection criteria 165

    Statistical significance of the tables 165

    Companies included in this survey 166